development
girl

doubleday
new york london toronto
sydney auckland

development girl

girl

the hollywood
virgin's guide
to making it in the
movie business

by hadley davis

A MAIN STREET BOOK

PUBLISHED BY DOUBLEDAY
a division of Random House, Inc.
1540 Broadway, New York, New York 10036

MAIN STREET BOOKS, DOUBLEDAY, and the
portrayal of a building with a tree are
trademarks of Doubleday, a division of
Random House, Inc.

Book design by Laurie Jewell
Illustration by Meredith Hamilton

Library of Congress Cataloging-in-Publication Data
Davis, Hadley.
Development girl: the Hollywood virgin's guide
to making it in the movie business / Hadley
Davis. — 1st ed.
p.   cm.
"A Main Street book."
1. Motion pictures—Vocational guidance—
United States. 1. Title.
PN1995.9.P75 D38
791.43'02'93—dc21
98-48443
CIP

ISBN 0-385-49431-9
Printed in the United States of America
June 1999
First Edition
10 9 8 7 6 5 4 3 2 1

For Nana and Papa,
Bev and Bill,
who hooked me
on showbiz.

Thank you to:
Susan Cartsonis, Marlene Adelstein,
Pam McCarthy, and Judy Tobey for
giving me my break(s). A special
shout out to ICM's Karen Gerwin,
agent extrodinaire. Denell Downum
of Doubleday (talk about a D-girl)
for stepping up. Marisa Acocella,
reigning queen of power babe-ness.
Jane D. for her freelance editing
and TLC. Jon D. for his bargain
legal advice and TLC. Carrie D.,
BFF. Lara Shriftman for her perpet-
ual, perfect, plugs. Sherri Cooper,
chief cheerleader. Jane Long, the
original smart-girl. Cohort Bonnie
Schneider for reminding me that
I was never meant to be "a supporting character in someone else's
sleeper." The one and only Adriana
Trigiani—thank God *you* were born.

Development Girl also thanks:
Christina Semmel, Craig Gering,
Renee Witt, Kyle Heller, Amanda Klein,
Michelle Raimo, Jennifer Berman,
Annalise Carol, Amie Steir, Ruthanna
Hopper, Jake Spitz, Lauren Flynn,
Sarah Goldman, Drew Reed, Jon Ein,
Jenna Cooper, Justin Evans, Kit
Golden, Jimmy Hurley, Jill Cutler,
Lisa Harrison, Stacey Pashcow,
Michelle Press, Heather Zeegen,
Jay Mandel, Chris Durian, Gwen
Lighter, Lewis Canfield, Doug
Hilton, Emily Fox, Al Perry, Chris
Manning, and Mandy Stein.

contents

foreword

Read bestselling books for a living. Watch films for money. Go to see Broadway plays for work. Socialize at premiere parties for pay.

I am a movie "Development girl," and, believe it or not, this is my job description. Do you think my career sounds fabulous and fun? Well, you aren't alone.

Ever since I started "in the business"—show business, that is—everyone I know—and many I don't—has come knocking at my door. In fact, if I had a dollar for every ounce of advice I've given away free in the last few years, I'd be rich (or at least own a pair of Manolo Blahnik shoes)! The requests for "informational interviews" from college graduates and undergrads, MBA's, lawyers, friends of friends, parents' friends' kids, peers' siblings, you name it, have been staggering. Letters have come from strangers, questions from audience members attending the panels I've served on. What does it mean to be in "Development"? How do you become a movie executive? How do you break into the business? Is your job as glamorous as it seems? They've wanted to know what my life is like. They are looking for a window into a career path that is not as easily imaginable as that of doctor, lawyer, architect, or professor.

I found that I had lots and lots of advice to give—advice resulting from my adventures in "the industry" working for both a major studio and production companies—and too little time to fill all of the requests.

So I decided to write it all down, and *Development Girl:*

The Hollywood Virgin's Guide to Making It in the Movie Business is the result. This is a guidebook I wish *I* had had when I was graduating and job/career hunting. Designed for those interested in the business of film (rather than in becoming a writer or director), this is a pragmatic approach to the industry—to landing and keeping a job and to understanding what it really takes to become a young executive on the rise in Hollywood.

And, by the way, "Hollywood" is not about a place. It's about an institution, a club, a way of life, a state of mind. In order to belong, you must know its language, its code, its lingo.

If getting into bed with a director, making a pass to an agent, and being picked up by a distributor sound to you like X-rated activities, then you, my dear, are a Hollywood Virgin. But don't despair. This is your book. Within these pages lie the tricks of the trade—from *the* trades to the schmooze to the pitch. Read on and you'll learn not only how to talk the Tinseltown talk but what to wear, where to work, and whom to date. And in no time you'll be prepared to play with the players.

—Hadley Davis, May *1999*

development
girl

who's that d-girl?
(or guy)

Who wouldn't want to
be a D-Girl or Guy?
Here's a glimpse at the
Wonderful World of
Development.

I'm just so tired, Billy. I never thought
I'd be so tired at twenty-two. . . .

—Demi Moore in **St. Elmo's Fire**

d is for development

According to Mr. Webster, "to develop" is to grow, to expand, or to unfold. Film develops. We girls wait and wait to develop. God, how I waited! And of course we must be careful about the reputation we develop. But that's development in the real world. The entertainment world is another story. . . .

In the movie biz, Development is a film's odyssey from first draft to production. It is the process by which a motion picture is conceived, nurtured, and brought to life. And just like a young thing blossoming into womanhood, the Development process can sometimes take years.

Those who work in Development for studios or production companies find concepts or screenplays or **manuscript**s* or books or plays or magazine articles or

On the D tip:

A D-Girl or Guy knows who the next hot young thing will be, who can't get arrested—and who just has for real.

---

* Words and phrases in boldface are explained in the Glossary beginning on page 169.

pitches that they think will make for stellar cinematic fare. Basically that means their job is to find the movie in any story. The search is an arduous one, involving lots of reading and lots of time. There is a ton of bad stuff out there to sift through and reject. On a bad day the process of finding a good movie project is like looking for a needle in a haystack. In David Mamet's play *Speed-the-Plow* (the one that starred Madonna on Broadway in the eighties), a movie producer laments, "If it's not quite 'Art' and not quite 'Entertainment,' it's here on my desk." I, however, have always preferred to think of my search for the next wildly popular action-adventure blockbuster, period romance, legal thriller, or whatever as a treasure hunt.

Once a great movie story has been uncovered, Development staff must find appropriate screenwriters to scribe the perfect screenplay. They must also find the right director and actors to carry out the vision.

Development is a precarious and vulnerable process. If any piece of the puzzle (writer, director, actor) backs out or fails to live up to expectations, the entire project can be thrust into **Development hell** or simply fall apart.

At the end of the day, when a project is finally given the **green light** to move into production, the Development staff must let go and let the chosen **talent** go make their movie. And no matter how well they've done their job, they never know how the picture will turn out artistically or in the **box office** (kind of like how you can't predict your eventual chest size).

the delight of development

So what's it like being a "D"? Take us to a cocktail party and we can talk about Wally Lamb's next bestseller that we've read seven months before it hits the bookstore and eight before it gets Oprah's blessing. We've already seen a screening of a small film you just might hear about at Oscar time. And the latest Broadway hit? Well, we attended a workshop last summer at a dingy basement space between Ninth and Tenth avenues. . . . Oh, yes, the film rights have already been **option**ed. We can tell you who the next hot young thing will be, who can't get arrested—and who just has for real.

What can I say? We Development Girls (and Development Guys) are decidedly in the know. We're hooked in. We're hooked up. It's cool being one of the cultural cognoscenti. But even cooler is the rare evening of transformation—an epiphany of a play, a magical movie, a student film that makes me laugh, a **script** that brings me to the verge of tears. These are the moments of artistic truth that lift me out of my daily grind, my latest boy troubles, the five pounds I am forever trying to lose, or my ongoing anxiety over cancer and global warming and earthquakes. And these are the soul-gratifying times when I've nearly pinched myself: "This is a job—*my* job!"

Discussing the richness of a novelist's writing, the depth of a script's characters, the nuances of theme, what the work has to say about the human experience—all these often make a typical **weekend read** meeting feel like a literature class. Being part of the creative process by helping a writer to really nail a script (and finding your **script notes** incorporated into a screenplay) is also immensely gratifying.

Although not every film project is an intensely intellectual exercise, each is a quick in-depth study—often of a subject I know nothing about. After all, the subjects of movies are diverse—from Shakespeare to tornadoes, from space travel to fly-fishing.

Perhaps the most rewarding part of my job, however, is working with and getting to know writers and directors, some of whom are brilliant or hysterical or bizarre or endearing or visionary, some of whom I have forged relationships of mutual respect and admiration with, some of whom I have come to call friends.

my so-called life

There is a price to pay for being so *au courant*. Unfortunately, there is more very, very bad material than anything else. The quantity of trash you'll have to waste hours on is astounding. You can't fathom the number of sadistic slashers, sicko serial killers, and scuzzy S&M addicts I've met in scripts over the years. Monday's mood doesn't call for a maudlin murder mystery? Sorry! Got a friend's birthday bash Thursday? Oh, well! Instead you have to peruse the new Judith Krantz (who, by the way, compared to Monday's mystery scribe, is a regular Hemingway).

When there is finally a decidedly decent document on the docket, you must read it at an outrageous pace. Stephen King might make good beach reading, but try schlepping home a seven-hundred-page manuscript for the weekend. Not a fun Saturday night!

At least you can suffer with a torturous manuscript in the comfort of your own home. In my experience nothing is quite as horrid as being antsy, hot, and hungry because it is 10 P.M. and you've gone to a deplorably dull **reading** directly from the office without dinner and all you want is to be on your couch with some Ben & Jerry's Chocolate Chip Cookie Dough and *Mary Tyler Moore* reruns.

You don't get paid overtime in Development, but the life of a D is a bizzy, busy twenty-four/seven. In fact, there is no way to "turn off your job"; there is always another script to skim, and there might be a movie in the *Dateline* segment you're watching from the Stairmaster or the germ of an idea in the newspaper you're looking at on the subway or a jumping-off point for a romantic comedy in a magazine story you are perusing as your pedicure dries.

P.S.: Although I often have eaten dinner at 11 P.M., popped three Tylenol, and fallen asleep with paper strewn about me, I could never imagine doing anything else!

the biz

(there's no business like . . .)

They've said it before, but I've gotta say it again. There's simply "no business like show business." So you wanna be in the movie business? You need a crash course on the basics. Here ya go.

D-girl: I'm sorry, but I just didn't think your script was any good. I found it flat and trite.

Screenwriter: Exactly what kind of material do you recommend? James Joyce? Dostoyevsky? . . . You would have turned down *Gone With the Wind*!

Studio executive: That was me. I said, "Who wants to see a Civil War picture?"

—From Billy Wilder's **Sunset Boulevard**

the development of the "development girl"

Development Girl or D-Girl is a term that originated back in the day when the only jobs for women in the movie business ness were in the **story department**s of studios. Women were "script girls"—the West Coast equivalent of the New York publishing or magazine jobs for young, literary-minded females fresh out of Radcliffe. They were allowed to deal with the ideas, the words, and the writers, but not the business per se. The "girl" part of the title, derived from a sexist Hollywood boys' club, spoke of their subordinate position in the studio system vis-à-vis men.

Well, we've come a long way, baby. Women climb the ranks and in many cases are the ranks or run the ranks. Almost half of the Hollywood studios are headed by women, giving ladies the ultimate power—the authority to **green-light** films. There are Power Babes at the helm of Paramount (Sherry Lansing), Fox 2000 (Laura Ziskin), Universal (Stacey Snider), Columbia (Amy Pascal),

On the D tip:

D-Guys or Gals might sell their souls to get the next big project for their studio.

DreamWorks (Laurie McDonald), and United Artists (Lindsay Doran).

Nevertheless, the D-Girl label has stuck. I think of the term affectionately. It's kind of retro-hip. Anyway, the whole woman thing is a drag and makes me feel old—I'd much rather be an eternal girl.

Today a boy can be a D-Girl (how's that for equality?). In fact, there are just as many D-Guys as Gals, and, I might add, they do their job just as effectively. The term now connotes a smart young twenty-something on the rise, on a playing field somewhere between an assistant and an executive. It is a great place to be. These fledgling **player**s are the radar, the eyes and ears of the industry, and are truly relied on by their executive superiors. Their youth—and the energy, trend-consciousness, and innate understanding of pop culture that this youth implies—is regarded as an asset. It is the D's job to be hooked in with the community of other D-People and **agents. Buzz** about new writers, directors, and scripts is their invaluable commodity and currency. To get **hot** information and trade it for more hype, D's must **track,** socialize, network, **schmooze,** and work the phones. They must be armed with gossip. They must do **favor**s and be owed favors. They must be charming. They must be busybodies (in a classy way, of course).

D's have paid their dues as assistants; they have paid dearly for their status (such as it is). It is not surprising, then, that they tend to be profoundly ambitious, determined, and single-minded. It is commonly thought that D-Guys or Gals might sell their souls to learn about or get the next big project for their company. I will neither confirm nor deny—this may or may not be true. What is certain, however, is that they are a hungry bunch (D-Girls eat a lot of salad), and they work very, very hard.

executive 101

Here's a breakdown of positions at studios and production companies:

Power Babes and Big Boys, aka Executives
President
Senior vice president
Vice president

D-Guys and Girls, aka Junior Executives
Director of Development
Creative executive (CE)
Creative associate
Story editor

Slaves, aka Assistants
Creative assistant
Executive assistant
Personal assistant
Intern

Executives often receive a producer credit for projects they find and/or shepherd. Occasionally D's also receive such a producer or **associate producer** title.

The time it takes to ascend in the biz from slave to Power Babe varies, but quick climbs are not at all unusual. In fact, a twenty-eight-year-old senior vice president is not a rarity.

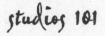

studios 101

Studios are the money, marketing, and management machines that get commercial pictures made. There are **the majors**—Columbia Pictures, DreamWorks SKG, Walt Disney Company, 20th Century–Fox, Universal Pictures, Paramount Pictures, and Warner Brothers—as well as Polygram Filmed Entertainment, MGM/United Artists, New Line Cinema, and Castle Rock Entertainment. Some of these studios own and operate different divisions with each functioning autonomously and specializing in releasing certain types of films. For example, Fox has 20th Century–Fox ("big Fox"), Fox Family Films, Fox Searchlight, and Fox 2000. 20th Century–Fox films produces broad **commercial** films—comedies (*There's Something About Mary*), dramas (*Titanic*), and slick, **high-concept,** action-packed flicks (*The Siege*); Fox Searchlight has a more **indie** mission producing films like *The Ice Storm* and also acquiring films to distribute such as *The Full Monty*; while Fox 2000 has a more pop charge with a female bent à la *Brokedown Palace.*

As the sponsors of motion pictures, studios get the last word from beginning to end. A senior studio exec decides what projects to buy and when a script is ready to go into production and also (except in rare cases) has final cut in the editing room—meaning the studio reserves the right to change a film's last scene or first scene or any scene in between.

production companies 101

Money defines the relationship between studios and production companies. A production company typically has a deal with a particular studio (unless it is led by an independent **producer**). Although very bare-bones **housekeeping deal**s exist, a studio deal usually means that a studio finances the production company—pays the salary of employees, the rent, all overhead—and, when the studio chooses, funds the production company's films. Such production-company/studio deals come in the form of either first-look deals or exclusive deals. A first-look deal means that when a production company wants to develop a project, they present the project to the studio. If the studio isn't interested in the project and passes, the production company is allowed to **shop** the project around to any other studio. If a production company has an exclusive deal with a studio, they are not allowed to bring the project elsewhere. The production company does not pursue the project further. Either way, it sounds like a good arrangement for the production company, right? So what's in it for the studio?

Production companies are created and driven by a star, director, writer/director, or producer. For the studio, having a deal with a production company is a way to guarantee that it will have the opportunity to be in business with that individual and reap the benefits of her or his box-office appeal, directorial talent, reputation, eye for material, track record of blockbuster hits, etc. These deals mean that production companies' development executives constantly bring projects to the studios' development executives, providing them with a continuous flow of product. These production arrangements are negotiated for a specific period of time—months or years—after which the deal may (or may not) be **re-up**ped.

Here are some examples of production companies and the studios at which they currently reside:

Twinkle, Twinkle—Celebs

Star: Julia (Roberts)
Production company: Shoelace Productions
Deal: Disney/Touchstone Pictures

Star: Alicia (Silverstone)
Production company: First Kiss Productions

Deal: Columbia Pictures

Star: Tom (Cruise)
Production company: CW Productions
Deal: Paramount

Star: Meg (Ryan)
Production company: Prufrock Pictures
Deal: Castle Rock

Star: Chris (O'Donnell)
Production company: George Street
Productions
Deal: Warner Brothers

Star: Michael (Douglas)
Production company: Furthur Films
Deal: Universal

Star: Nicolas (Cage)
Production company: Saturn Films
Deal: Disney

Star: Robert (Redford)
Production company: Southfork Pictures
Deal: Disney

Cut!—Directors

Director: Marty (Scorsese)
Production company: Cappa Productions
Deal: Disney

Director: Oliver (Stone)
Production company: Illusion Entertainment Group
Deal: Cinergi Pictures

Director: Penny (Marshall)
Production company: Parkway Productions
Deal: Universal Pictures

Director: Spike (Lee)
Production company: 40 Acres and a Mule
Deal: Columbia Pictures

Director: Quentin (Tarantino)
Production company: A Band Apart
Deal: Miramax

Director: Chris (Columbus)
Production company: 1492 Pictures
Deal: 20th Century–Fox

Director: Barbra (Streisand)
Production company: Barwood
Deal: Columbia Pictures

Director: Michael (Bay)
Production company: Bay Films
Deal: Disney

Director: James (Brooks)
Production company: Gracie Films
Deal: Columbia

Director: Amy (Heckerling)

Production company: Heckerling-Caplan
Deal: Paramount

Director: Ron (Howard)
Production company: Imagine Entertainment
Deal: Universal

Love Ya, Babe—Producers

Producer: Scott Rudin
Production company: Scott Rudin Productions
Deal: Paramount
(The Truman Show)

Producer: Deborah Schindler
Production company: Deborah Schindler
   Productions
Deal: Warner Brothers
(How Stella Got Her Groove Back)

Producer: Jerry Bruckheimer
Production company: Jerry Bruckheimer Films
Deal: Disney
(Armageddon)

Mr. And Mrs. Producer: Arnold and Anne Kopelson
Production company: Kopelson Entertainment
Deal: 20th Century–Fox
(A Perfect Murder)

Producer: Denise Di Novi
Production company: Di Novi Pictures

Deal: Warner Brothers
(Practical Magic)

Producer: Larry Mark
Production company: Laurence Mark Prods.
Deal: Disney
(Romy and Michelle's High School Reunion)

Mr. And Mrs. Producer: Kenneth "Babyface" and
   Tracey Edmonds
Production company: Edmonds Entertainment
Deal: Fox 2000
(Soul Food)

projects 101

So how do the D's at studios and production companies
work together? A **script** is submitted **officially** to a production company by an agent. It is then **cover**ed by a
reader and read or skimmed by an intern, assistant,
D-Girl, D-Guy, Big Boy, or Power Babe in the office. Who
reads the script depends on how important it is. For example, an intern may be asked to take a look at a screenplay for the company as a **courtesy read.** In other
words, the script is perused as a favor because it was
penned by Spielberg's podiatrist's cousin. The senior VP,
however, will be the one taking home the new book by
John Grisham or Mario Puzo.

Speaking of Mario Puzo, let's suppose Popcorn Productions' **coverage** on his latest family epic, *The Godmother,* is strong and so is the production prez's resolve to add this project to her development **slate** (once she hears that Mira Sorvino is **attached** to play the Godmother's God-daughter's Godsister). So she brings the book into the studio. Popcorn has a first-look deal at Fox, and the prez decides to give the book to an exec at Fox 2000, reasoning that the studio arm will be eager to work with a young, sought-after actress like Mira. She describes the project as *The Godfather* **meets** *Waiting to Exhale.* The **hook** is that it's an all-gal, Italian-American ensemble piece with rich dramatic roles sure to appeal to several **A-list** actresses.

A studio VP reads the coverage and the first fifty pages of the novel and flips for it. Hearing that Jujy Fruit Productions has **brought** the project **in** at a rival studio, he places a **preemptive bid** to buy the project for Popcorn immediately. It's sold for a mid-six figures **against** a very high six figures (nearly seven). The project enters the studio's **pipeline.**

Popcorn Productions now must find a screenwriter to transform the book into a screenplay. A D compiles a list of **available** scribes emanating Hollywood **heat.** An exec combs through the list, eliminates and adds names. Popcorn's number-one pick, clutch hitter Ron Bass, renowned for home runs like *The Joy Luck Club* and *Rain Man,* is drafted for the job. Once a writer has committed, it is time to start attaching stars and a director. Again a D compiles a company wish list. **Meeting**s are taken. Cher becomes attached to star as the Godmother, Demi

Moore commits to be the Goddaughter. Meanwhile, fresh off of *I Know What You Did Last Fall,* Kevin Williamson signs a **pay-or-play** directing deal.

By now three months have gone by, and the first draft is **delivered.** The entire office will read the screenplay, and each member of the staff writes script notes citing ways to **punch up** the writing. These notes are compiled by a D-Girl or Guy and presented to the writer. Development is under way. A handful of **rewrite**s, three **script doctor**s, and a **polish** later, the script will be good to go.

office politics 101: the food chain

The Hollywood Development office is not unlike the earth's dietary procession, in which each life form consumes lower members of the chain and is in turn more or less preyed upon by higher members.

Let's suppose an assistant or a D finds a script or pitch he really likes the taste of. He'll show it to an executive. She chews on it. If she thinks it satisfying, she'll present it to the president. The president will be the one with the ultimate authority to decide whether or not to commit to placing the particular project on the company menu.

As I see it, the higher up you land in the hierarchy . . .

1. The less chance you have of someone else above you taking credit for your "find"—or ingesting *your* catch, if you will.

2. The more dough you've got (assistants can make $20,000 to $40,000, D's $40,000 to about $75,000, VPs $75,000 to $100,000 and up and up and up).

3. The better fed you are, literally—thanks to the benefit of your unlimited expense account. (Sometimes assistants have limited expense accounts; D's can take people out to lunch, dinner, drinks, plays, etc., on the company— but execs tend to really live it up without consequence.)

4. The more assistants you have to order your cappuccinos, make your restaurant reservations—you name it.

l.a.
(versus nyc)

Now that you know
something about the
jobs out there, you've
gotta figure out where
to live. What are the
realities, the myths,
the stereotypes, the
hardships, and the
benefits of being in the
business in the "City
of Angels" versus
"Hollywood on the
Hudson"? Must you
"go West" to work
"in Hollywood"? Yes
and no . . .

I live in Los Angeles . . . that is to say I was deeply unhappy but I didn't know it because I was so happy all the time. . . .

—Steve Martin, **L.A. Story**

go west, young thang

The epicenter of the entertainment-business universe is L.A. Los Angeles is where the studios are located and where the majority of films are shot. It is, of course, where the stars reside.

L.A. is also where the moguls preside. The powers that be are based on the West Coast. So L.A. is where decisions and deals are made. The offices are the snazziest. The jobs are in greatest abundance.

Those jobs generally offer a broad base of experience and the chance to be involved in the entire process of conceiving a motion picture from idea to script to production to silver screen. As a result, Hollywood is where careers are built—and built the fastest.

On the D tip:

Becoming a player is in part looking, acting, and yes, *playing* the part . . . . Isn't that fabulously democratic?

How serious are you about the entertainment business? Are you ready to eat, sleep, and breathe it? What cars are to Detroit, what country music is to Nashville, what software is to Seattle, movies are to L.A. Los Angeles is a one-industry town. Los Angelenos are consumed by, steeped in the world of film. Whether you're at the grocery store in Santa Monica or the doctor's office in Beverly Hills, everyone in line seems to be talking about the screenplay they're writing; everyone in the waiting room seems to be reading *Variety*. Over chopped salad at the Ivy or a *Hawaii Five-O* fruit smoothy at the Newsroom Café it's wise to look over one's shoulder and to either side before gossiping about a boss—these words are sure to be heard by a friend of an acquaintance of the object of your chatter.

In a business that operates on personal relationships, there's no better place to make showbiz friends—and lots of 'em. When so many are in some way or another involved in the same industry, there is an automatic thread, tie, commonality, sense of community even. In assistant days, when life can resemble boot camp, it is important to have peers to commiserate with, who understand the particular hardship suffered. (But L.A. comrades are also after the same opportunities—maybe even the same promotion. Be warned: These sympathetic ears can be competitive and cutthroat, too.)

bicoastal blues

Most studios do have satellite development offices in New York (Universal, Paramount, Columbia Pictures, New Line Cinema, and Disney all have NYC offices). These offices, however, are usually tiny on the creative end, consisting of just a few people, and serve a different purpose than the headquarters. In general, L.A.'s focus is **spec**s, screenplays, pitches, and production. And because NYC is the country's publishing-industry and theater capital, New York is oriented toward books, magazines, and plays.

So here's how NYC and L.A. tend to interact. A New York satellite office procures the latest "big book" in manuscript form from an agent or on the sly, on a **slip** through an editor friend or even in a **trade** with another film company. A big book might be the latest novel by a big-time author whose books habitually sell to the movies—Elmore Leonard, for example. Or it could be a first-time author's work, just purchased by a publisher for a holy fortune and therefore creating quite a stir. Okay, so the big book arrives. An assistant Xeroxes the volume. Then the New York exec reads the text, and a reader is hired to write coverage. The L.A. office is alerted of the book's filmworthiness. Depending on the urgency (e.g., is there interest from competition? are there other bids on the table?), the manuscript and coverage will be FedExed or faxed page by page (by some unlucky intern) to Tinseltown. The West Coast office makes the final decision. If the studio chooses to buy the **rights** to the book, execs in L.A. do the negotiating and later attach the talent. In a year or two or five the New York office is invited to a screening of the film adaptation of the book they found. But mind you, those New Yorkers will have had little or no involvement in the development process.

new york state of mind

Although they can rattle off the reasons for their geographical choice, New Yorkers in film are painfully aware of inevitable trade-offs. Not only are fewer jobs to be had at every level in the Apple, but job instability is rampant. New York offices (for non–New York–based companies) are considered a luxury. This is especially true for production companies. When a production company has a great year or a lucrative hit or lands a generous new studio deal, it very likely may open a New York office. Well, when that company has a not-so-great year or when the studio deal expires, the New York office is the first to go. NYC offices therefore are constantly opening and closing. In the event that you eventually wind up at such an office, here are some signs of imminent downsizing to look for:

First: The morning muffin and bagel tray disappear.

Then: The Evian mineral water is replaced by Poland Spring.

Next up: Faithful readers are dismissed. (Result: You must lug home more scripts than ever.)

The End: The announcement that (surprise!) the office is closing.

Alas, perhaps I have painted too dark a portrait of the film biz in New York. There *is* more to moviemaking in the Apple than studio back offices. Producing in Manhattan is, in fact, more viable than ever. This is thanks in large part to the mega-successful, pseudo-independent film company–cum–studio (Disney-owned) Miramax, which has evolved and expanded and thrived and prospered in New York. Miramax produces about thirty-five films a year (while the typical Hollywood studio has scaled back to about seventeen a year). Not only has Miramax cornered the market on art-house, foreign, and edgy films, which showcase new talent and lap up Oscars, but their Dimension division, producers of *Scream,* has awakened Hollywood to the shrieking voice of the ever-growing teenybopper dollar. Similarly, former indie company October Films *(Secrets & Lies)* now owned by Universal, develops and acquires films from its New York base. These entities, along with The Shooting Gallery *(Sling Blade),* and a slew of smaller producers around town, have given NYC a movie-biz identity uniquely its own.

New York filmmakers like Ted Demme *(Rounders),* Todd Solondz *(Happiness),* Kevin Smith *(Chasing Amy),* Ed Burns *(She's the One),* and Gregg Mottola *(The Day Trippers)* to name a few, are not known for broad comedies or action-packed blockbusters with $100 million price tags. Instead, they shoot on a smaller scale, with a lower budget, and the result is often hipper and more controversial than typical Hollywood fare. If you land a gig working for one of these indie-flavored NYC companies you will indeed be in the thick of putting a picture together. It's good work if you can get it.

quality of life: a debate

A predicament particular to Los Angeles is the pervasiveness of the biz. Since the average citizen is a producer, an agent, an exec, a screenwriter, director, or actress (and, if not, they're a *wannabe* producer, agent, exec, screenwriter, director or actress), the biz can become all you can talk about and do talk about. There *is* no escape from work, some note, making L.A. life one-dimensional.

But ah, why complain when you've got those perpetually sunny skies, warm weather, the beach, a ride, a house in the Hills—a quality of life that can't be rivaled (and that life is, in general, decidedly more affordable). With low starting salaries (as low as the twenties), on both coasts, it's important to note that in L.A. rentals are cheaper and more spacious (room for roommates). And yup, just like on *Melrose Place* there are start-up apartment buildings with pools!

New Yorkers in the movie business adamantly argue that their quality of life is far superior. They will even insist on this notion in the middle of a blizzardy January, while holed up in a dingy one-room walk-up apartment, with careers advancing at a snail's pace compared to their counterparts on the left coast. These Manhattan diehards claim to require the cultural infusion of a Lincoln Center ballet, a gritty off-Broadway show, a smoky downtown bar. They emphasize the grounding import of a diverse circle of friends who include investment bankers, *Village Voice* reporters, and Web designers. And secretly they enjoy being the anomaly—the one kid on the block with the cool cinema vocation. They have consciously made a decision not to live "out there."

the scene: whose list are you on?

"What a fascinating comparison!" you exclaim, but what about the *important* stuff—the scene, the parties, the premieres, the people, the players—in each respective city? "Are the stereotypes true?" you inquire. In a word—absolutely!

There is a Young Hollywood Party every weekend in L.A. A house of entertainment roomies—**Endeavor Agency**'s trendiest turkette, a smart screenwriteress, a darling D. On Saturday word spreads from Brentwood to Los Feliz. By evening, twenty-somethings all over town have the address of the schmoozefest. The biz kids hang inside and out, drink, smoke (anything and everything), meet and greet their circle's latest arrivals. The fete always provides Monday-morning intrigue and innuendo. Two rival agents had a fistfight . . . a prodigy-producer hooked up with his assistant, etc.

There is no such social staple in NYC. Perhaps in part because apartments are too small for entertaining and in part because the city showbiz scene is more fragmented. Groups of friends (who may or may not be in the business) are more likely to meet up at a restaurant and move on to a club late at night.

The people who run the entertainment business run the L.A. see-and-be-seen scene. Who you are—i.e. your place in the social stratum—is determined by your job, which equals your power. In other words, Hollywood directors, executives, or flavors of the week have carte blanche. But, of course, most simply *aspire* to play with the players. Those reaching for the upper echelons are quite obsessed with what others think, placing great weight on the right car *(any* BMW is not sufficient; it must be the right color and right number) and on being noticed with (or better, on the arm of) the right up-and-comer(s) du jour. These wannabes are not dumb. Perception is the name of the game. Becoming a player is in part looking, acting, and yes, *playing* the part. . . . Isn't that fabulously democratic?

No such luck in New York, a town dominated by uptown Wall Street titans and downtown literati, not movie moguls. In Manhattan, producers are not socialites. Bona fide socialites are socialites.

At NYC premieres the entertainment elite mix and mingle with the power brokers from worlds ranging from finance to fashion. New York openings are notoriously low-key. A red-carpet screening is generally followed by dinner or drinks at a space taken over for the night. Dress is very much anything-goes.

In L.A., though, they get out the gowns and pull out all the stops. Flashy and splashy all the way. Celebs galore arrive to be photographed. And the glitterati come out full force. If the film is an **event movie,** the flick might even be followed by a theme-oriented, tented, shindig on the studio lot, replete with anything from fireworks and air shows to carnival rides. The cost of the occasion can easily run $500,000 plus (versus an average $50,000 for a typical New York affair).

That about covers it, sea to shining sea. But before you pick a coast, turn the page for a few more random details to keep in mind.

Livin' as a D in L.A. Versus NYC

	L.A.	NYC
Status symbols	Celebrity pal	Playwright pal
Ultimate publicity	*Hollywood Reporter's* "The Great Life."	*NY Post's* "Page Six."
Transport	Assistant: Used Jeep	Assistant: Subway MetroCard.
	Graduate to: New trucky car. Range Rover or Mercedes M-class.	Graduate to: Cab.
Bedside reading	Coverage.	New novel by previous week's featured Charlie Rose guest.
1:00 P.M. power lunch	Mr. Chow, Chaya Brasserie, The Grill, Spago, Barney Greengrass, Morton's, any studio-lot commissary.	5757 (Four Seasons), Brooklyn Diner USA, Fred's at Barneys, Bubby's, Tribeca Grill, Michael's.
Movie liked recently	Whatever opened biggest at the box office last weekend.	A flick "you probably didn't see" (because no one did!). "But the writer is really brilliant, and I wanted the L.A. office to buy the script, but they wouldn't listen to me."

Livin' as a D in L.A. Versus NYC

	L.A.	NYC
Idea of relaxation	Reading a script on the beach.	Reading a script in Sheep Meadow, Central Park.
Summer getaway weekend	House-sitting weekend at your friends' boss's boyfriend's house in Malibu.	At your boss's house in the Hamptons, where invited guests at dinner include neighbors Mr. and Mrs. Alec Baldwin.
Home sweet home	House shared with old college roommates in Silverlake.	Three-hundred-square-foot studio apartment on East Ninth street.
Stargazing	Spotted when pulled up next to you at a light: any one of the Planet Hollywood investors.	Spotted shopping at the Union Square Farmers' market: the latest couple to fall head over heels on the last Miramax movie set and subsequently buy a loft in the West Village.
Shopping trip	Jaunt to Fred Segal Santa Monica or Melrose.	Excursion to Scoop, Soho, or Upper East Side.

Livin' as a D in L.A. Versus NYC

	L.A.	NYC
Workout	The steps by the beach in Santa Monica.	The stairs to your fifth-floor walk-up.
Favorite hot restaurant	Anything so new it hasn't opened yet.	Anything so new it hasn't opened yet.
Typical premiere	Jim Carrey's latest.	Christina Ricci's latest.
Sweet treat	Red Vine licorice.	Chuba Chups pops.
Drug	X (Ecstasy).	P (Prozac).
Drink	Ice Blended from the Coffee Bean & Tea Leaf.	Absolut vodka martinini or Tanqueray cosmo.
Where to See and Be Seen	Billy Blank's Tae-Bo (workout), Yogatopia (Brentwood), The Polo Lounge (at Beverly Hills Hotel), Les Deux Cafés (restaurant), MTV Movie Awards, Dominick's, Four Seasons (for brunch), CAA's Christmas party, Kabbalah class, courtside at a Lakers game, ICM agent Ed Limato's annual Oscar-eve party.	Mercer Kitchen, Nobu, Indochine, Moomba (restaurants), spring fashion shows, Peggy Siegel (publicist) "word of mouth" screening, publicity launch party (for any book, fragrance, restaurant, or club), the Met's December Costume Institute Gala, Interscope's Ted Field's annual Fourth of July Hamptons bash, anywhere Leo is.

Livin' as a D in L.A. Versus NYC

	L.A.	NYC
Favorite causes	Democrat with potential to be Lincoln Bedroom host.	Independent Film Project, Lincoln Center Film Society, friend's indie film.
Where to be on Oscar night	Dorothy Chandler Pavilion, *Vanity Fair* and Miramax after-parties.	*Entertainment Weekly*'s party at Elaine's.
Holidays observed	Day of Atonement, Day of Academy Awards.	Summer Fridays.
Choice hotels	(when in NYC): The Mercer, Four Seasons, St. Regis.	(when in L.A.): Chateau Marmont, Four Seasons, The Mondrian.
Halloween costume	Dead producer.	Dead movie star.
Ultimate Christmas vacation spot	Hawaii.	St. Bart's.
Cell phone of choice	Assistant: Motorola Star Tac. Graduate to: Motorola V Series.	Assistant: Pay phone. Graduate to: Nokia.

getting hired
(& not fired)

· · · · · · ·

When the late, legendary
Dawn Steel (who eventu-
ally became president of
Paramount Pictures and
then Columbia Pictures)
was offered her first job
in the movie biz by
Michael Eisner (then at
Paramount), she told
him, "I don't know any-
thing about movies." He
reportedly responded:
"Neither does anybody
else. Good-bye, good
luck, and break a leg!"
—From Dawn Steele's
*They Can Kill You, But
They Can't Eat You*

What do you need to
know to land and keep
your first job in Tinsel-
town? Well, what you
need to know has ab-
solutely nothing to do
with film.

Receptionist: Mr. Bellamy, this is Ms. Wells. She's here about the job.

Bellamy: She's too good-looking.

Receptionist: Mr. Bellamy, that's not fair!

Bellamy: I'll just get her broken in, and some insurance salesman will waltz up and marry her.

Ms. Wells: I'm already engaged.

Bellamy: See.

Ms. Wells: But I'm not going to marry him, and besides, lots of secretaries are married, aren't they?

Bellamy: Not in this office! Some days you'll have to work until midnight having dinner with me and a perspective client. I'll drink too much and won't remember a damn word the next morning. You'll have but one sherry and remember everything.

Ms. Wells: I love sherry, and I have an excellent memory . . . Mr. Bellamy, couldn't you please give me a trial?

Bellamy: All right. I'll try you out for one week, starting as of now.

—From **Valley of the Dolls**

cover letters and résumés

Movie executives are a hurried, harried bunch. Hiring an intern or an assistant is a task most focus on for no more than fifty seconds at a time—between calls. Cover letters therefore should be short and sweet. Cover letters should not provide an in-depth psychoanalysis of why movie-moguldom has been bubbling in your blood since toddlerhood. Please, save it for your shrink.

Here's a sample letter fit for a D:

> Dear Hadley,
> My name is Joe Intern. I am a junior at NYU film school. I am writing to inquire about the availability of fall internships at D-Girl Productions. Attached is a copy of my résumé.
> I will call you at the end of the week to follow up.
>
> Thanks,
> Joe

On the D tip:

Isn't the ex-stepson of your stepmother's decorator an exec at United Artists?

Résumés *should* be clear and concise. Résumés *should not* highlight every club you've ever belonged to and every good deed you've performed since kindergarten. Yes, I once received a résumé that actually listed the kindergarten the applicant had attended. I am sure it was a very fine, snooty kindergarten (he must have known his colors at an abnormally young age). Needless to say (after a few good giggles), the résumé landed in the trash can. This is obviously an extreme case, but the point is, it's better to have a sparse, spare résumé than an overdecorated one.

Education
College name
- your GPA (if it's good)
- your major or anticipated major
- list one or two activities only

High School name
- year of graduation
- list major awards only (like Merit Scholarship)

Experience
Internships and jobs
- list them and tersely state tasks

Personal
- Forget about it! No one gives a crap about your hobbies (unless one of them is Xeroxing!)

networking: six degrees of separation

When looking for employment, one has no choice but to rely on the kindness of strangers. However, strangers who owe you nothing are not always so kind. Especially strangers in the entertainment business, who tend to be constantly harassed by an endless stream of job seekers.

Your object must be to make these strangers less strange and thus more kind. After all, you don't want your résumé to be left lonely and lost in a pile, and you don't want your call left in call-sheet purgatory, forever unreturned. You must unearth your "six degrees of separation" with anyone in the biz.

Now, don't start whining. You mean Joe Roth (chairman, Walt Disney Studios) isn't your uncle? You didn't grow up with Amy *Redford* or Eric *Eisner?* Well, are you sure you've polled everyone in your family? Isn't the exstepson of your stepmother's decorator an exec at United Artists? My first interview ever was with a William Morris agent who had been in my grandfather's bunk at camp!

Another way of making strangers more familiar is through your high-school or college alumni network. As a D-Girl I've never thrown away the résumé of a struggling student from my alma mater. Your university's career office will have databases (usually organized by industry) containing the affiliations of graduates. Some high schools also keep such records.

In addition, don't disregard, say, a fraternity brother's older sister who is working as an assistant at a random production company. A contact at the lowest level can be even more helpful than one at the highest. Assistants are often most likely to know of entry-level openings.

informational interviews

Once you've got a couple of names, I beg you, do not waste them on "informational interviews." When executives take time out to squeeze you into their day and lend you sage wisdom, that meeting itself becomes the favor. In other words, executives will not be likely to follow up and follow through on helping to find you employment because they will feel as though they have already given you enough attention. Regardless of whether or not you are gainfully employed, you are already off their conscience. Informational interviews therefore seldom lead to jobs.

Instead, send a letter requesting a phone conversation with the exec "or anyone in his or her office" to hear of any contacts, ideas, or suggestions they might have. You are after information about openings. You need names. You need referrals. Who cares who gives them to you? Grant executives the opportunity to have someone else return the call. Make it easy for them. Make your request impossible to refuse.

Call to follow up a week later. Don't fret if you don't get through. Chances are you won't. This is not a post-date will-he-call-won't-he-call-can-I-call-if-he-doesn't-call-me-what-if-I-call-and-he-doesn't-call-back dilemma. In *this* case an unreturned call is *not* a personal rejection (how refreshing!). These are just supremely preoccupied people. Keep calling once a week. Be friendly. Be patient. Befriend the assistant. *Do not* let on how frustrated you are (these people owe you nothing!). *Do* call in the morning (before the day is in full swing). *Do not* be afraid to leave voice mail. *Do not* assume that your name will be recognized and remembered. *Do* always refresh the assistant (or voice-mail retriever's) memory. Restate who you are, why you are calling, what you are after—and happily volunteer to refax your letter and résumé if necessary. You must be tenacious not annoying. After a month of calling (four calls), move on.

interviewing

Hallelujah! You've got yourself a real interview! You're on your way—if you don't mess up. I'm gonna give it to you straight from mouth of a gal on the other side of the desk. Here's some of the stuff we D's want to hear:

"I just want to get my foot in the door."
"I will work my ass off."
"I am willing to do whatever it takes."

"I am meticulously organized."

"I am a fast and proficient typist."

"I am even-tempered and easy to be around."

"I will take scripts home to read."

"I am single and have no life." (This one worked to get me my first D job.)

When hiring an intern or assistant, I look for positive, enthusiastic energy. A go-getter vibe. A person who is delicately aggressive. The questions foremost on my mind are:

1. Will he "jump in," or will he need a ton of direction?
2. Will she have the common sense to anticipate work, activities, problems, and crises?
3. When he finishes a task, will he ask me what he can do next, or will he sit idly waiting for the next assignment?
4. Can she pick up the phone and articulately, politely handle situations with calm reason, or will she be easily fazed and frazzled?

internships

An unpaid internship is by far the best way into the business. As an intern you learn the ropes and make contacts that will lead to a paying job when the time is ripe. And

you do have your cool perks to write home about—
passes to screenings, hanging out on the **lot,** in-office
celebrity sightings.

Note: The very first day of my Warner Brothers internship, Warren Beatty (who had just moved on from
Madonna to Annette, mind you) installed himself in a
guest office across from my cubicle—and by the way, he
definitely checked me out. Later that summer, Quincy
Jones struck up a conversation while waiting for a meeting. We walked around the floor together, while he ID'ed
every obscure film still that donned the walls. Then there
was the elevator ride with Mr. Coppola, who informed
me that the Starbursts I was chewing were loaded with
sugar and bad things. I refrained from asking Francis
which of us needed most to consider waistline issues. Re-
grettably, my last intern only got up close and personal
with the likes of Steve Guttenberg (most recently of *It
Takes Two*—the Olsen twins' **vehicle**), whom an agent
had roped me into meeting with.

Interns work for assistants and D's copying scripts,
running errands, researching, typing correspondence, fil-
ing, ordering lunch, covering for the receptionist. If it
sounds like sucky grunt work, it sounds like an intern
task.

Unbelievably, these showbiz slaves aren't kidnapped
from the campuses of USC, UCLA, Columbia, and NYU.
Internships are actually competitive. At Kopelson Entertainment, where the senior vice president is a former in-

tern, candidates have to endure several rounds of interviews with execs, D's, and assistants alike and write sample coverage before gaining admittance to the plantation. Rest assured, they'll tell you after such grilling, the master—Arnold K. himself—will learn your name! You might even get a peek at his palatial quarters.

"Where do I sign up?" you yelp. Internships (surprise!) are much easier to find than paying full-time assistant jobs. Networking is not a necessity. Call 1-800-815-0503 and order *The Hollywood Creative Directory,* a seasonal listing of every production company and studio on both coasts—addresses, names, titles, and phone numbers. It'll cost you about fifty dollars, but it is an invaluable investment. When you get your hands on the (rightfully) self-proclaimed "Film and Television Industry Bible," turn to the "Studio Deals" section at the back. You'll find a listing of every studio and the production companies it's hooked up with. As a general rule, the companies with studio deals are the established and legitimate ones you should be contacting. Look up the companies, check out the movies they've made, and go ahead, make a wish list. Now call them up and ask to whom you would direct a letter regarding an internship.

If NYC or L.A. is not your native town (and contrary to popular industry belief, there *are* fifty states) an unpaid internship can be an expensive prospect. There's food and shelter and, in California, a car. Consider it summer school. At least you don't have to pay tuition. Try to find a long-lost friend or relative's couch or floor to crash on.

Otherwise, in L.A. try UCLA student housing. In New York call NYU or Columbia, where you can shack up reasonably. If Mummy and Daddy aren't coming through for you, remember, when there is free labor involved, negotiation is possible. Volunteer three days and temp for two. Leave at 5 P.M. each day for your waitress post.

It is one thing to place an internship on your résumé; it is quite another to parlay an internship into a paid position. I hired two interns because I couldn't live without them. I also fired two because I couldn't live with them. Don't think just because you aren't getting a paycheck you can't get canned. No intern is better than an intern with a chip on his shoulder. No intern is better than one who shows up only when she feels like it. Prove yourself reliable. Endear yourself. Forge friendships. Show 'em the best intern they've ever seen the likes of. Be the first to arrive and the last to leave. Take home scripts. In a business of make-believe, pretend you're making a quarter of a million dollars a year (at least!).

Another important way to make the most of your intern experience is to learn to write killer coverage. Coverage is a synopsis of a script, a page of comments (consisting of an opinion on the merits of the material) and a verdict for executives: "recommend" (you've got a huge hit on your hands), "consider" (some issues need to be addressed, but the material is strong enough for you to transform it into film), "maybe" (you should take a quick look at the script, but it's highly doubtful), or "pass" (I think this script totally sucks, and so will you). Coverage exists so that executives don't have to actually read material themselves. Study sample coverage, then take a crack at it yourself. Ask your D to edit your attempt. Try to cover at least a script a week during your tenure. Save these writing samples—you will need to submit them when applying for a real job down the line.

You may want to consider working for one company each summer, rotating execs or offices. If you choose to do so, try to install yourself at a growing company, where opportunity appears imminent. Pop your head into the human-resources department (if it exists). Introduce yourself. Personnel types are notoriously icky people, but they sure can be good buddies for the job searcher to have. Ingratiate yourself. With a little luck, a dreamy D-assistant slot at the targeted company will be your postgraduation destiny.

reading

If that assistant job doesn't pan out immediately working as a freelance reader is another valid way in and/or a way to support yourself during the job search. Readers are paid, per script, to write coverage.

The main character in David Hollander's play *The Sun Dialogues* is a reader. Here's how he introduces himself: "My name is Walter Blount. I read scripts for a living. For those of you who are unfamiliar with the film industry hierarchy, this means that I am one of the lowliest forms of human grist known to the Hollywood mill. . . . There are, however, two benefits to being a script reader: I get to sleep late and I get to sit around in my underwear all day."

There are other advantages to reading, though, one of which is that your written judgment of material usually lands right in the hands of execs and is in many cases the basis for their decision to reject (if not to purchase) a script.

There is pressure with such responsibility. A "consider" means that the exec will invest her time and read the script, a "pass" might mean she won't look at the material at all. If a reader is off base, this exec will *not* be happy. Therefore, a reader must judge material according to the criteria of those he's reading for (although another character in *The Sun Dialogues* claims to simply "count death scenes and depictions of heterosexual intercourse"—if the "combined total is less than five," he rejects the script).

Every studio and many, many production companies hire readers, and turnover is high. To get a reading client, it helps to be armed with real sample coverage from an internship. However, many companies will let you give it a whirl writing sample coverage as a tryout.

P.S.: Reading has been known to lead to full-time development employment. Sherry Lansing (chairman of Paramount) began as a script reader—and so did I.

the mailroom

What do Meryl Poster (co-president of production, Miramax), Barry Diller (chairman, Home Shopping Network and Universal TV), David Geffen (DreamWorks SKG co-founder), Bernie Brillstein (Brillstein-Grey), Jerry Weintraub (producer, *Diner*), Irwin Winkler (producer, *Goodfellas, Raging Bull, Rocky*), and Cary Woods (producer, *Scream, Godzilla, Kids, Copland*) have in common? They all "started in the mailroom." That is, they are graduates of the only official Hollywood master's-degree program(s). They have completed the boot-campish curriculum at one of the "big three" agencies—**William Morris Agency,** Creative Artists Agency (**CAA**), and International Creative Management (**ICM**).

An agency-trainee stint—at one of the above-mentioned companies or at the smaller United Talent Agency (**UTA**) or Endeavor Agency—is a very viable, highly recommended path to a movie-Development job. Many L.A. Development execs like to only hire assistants out of the agencies because they are so well versed in the inner workings of the industry.

To get the mailroom gig, however, you must swear up and down that the only thing you want to be when you grow up is an agent. After you write a letter of inquiry to the human-resources department at an agency, you will be contacted by phone or prescreened, then invited to interview, first with personnel and at the final stages with agents themselves. You will be given a typing test (possibly on an archaic typewriter!) and expected to hunt-and-peck fifty words a minute. Although only a peon hopeful, you will still be poked and prodded by the pros. One former trainee recalls enduring nine interviews in three days!

Depending on the agency, there will be from four to twenty mailroom inductees at a time, not including the lifers—a mailroom head who inevitably looks like some embalmed, failed actor, and his lackeys—Supply Guy and Xerox Guy. Trainees themselves sort and distribute letters and packages, schmoozing with agents and assistants, asking if there are any scripts they need read and covered, getting to know who's who, as they wheel their cart around the halls. In between runs they hang out in the mailroom, frequently fielding calls from agents' assistants requesting that someone buy a copy of the current issue of *Playboy* (for a movie review, of course), someone pick up Ivana Trump's laundry, someone else get lunch (McDonald's fries but a BK burger). Such and such muckety-muck needs his car serviced, and so-and-so star needs to be retrieved at the airport. About once a month trainees are invited to an after-work "talk" given by an agency client (director, writer, producer, and so on) on some aspect of the business.

Every company's mailroom operates differently. And within each company there are additional West Coast/East Coast variations. Habitually, however, the most senior trainee is the mailroom coordinator—the one who assigns these terrific tasks to her co-workers (and chooses which she will deign to perform herself). Generally, the last person to enter the mailroom is the last one to be promoted out of it.

In Los Angeles usually the following, intermediate phase of the training program is "Dispatch," which consists of tracking the messengering of packages to studios, production companies, actors, casting directors, sets, etc., during periodic trips to the Valley, Hollywood, Culver City, and West L.A. Before and after package policing, dispatchers daily assist assistants on "morning desk" or "evening desk" duty, during which time they learn how to answer and place phone calls properly for agents. At some agencies next up is the "Reading Room," where trainees literally sit and peruse scripts—and learn to write coverage. Essentially these trainees serve as in-house readers.

Finally a trainee is deemed a "floater." Now each day begins with dread. A floater is assigned to a particular agent or department (perhaps an assistant is sick or on vacation or an agent from the other coast's office is in town). You never know what lies in store—or whom you'll get stuck with. A floater could wind up at reception, the switchboard, PR, accounting, legal, business affairs, TV, or literary. He could find himself getting Katzenberg on the phone for the agency's president or Bruce Willis on the line for a "mo pic" (motion picture) talent broker. Occasionally a floater will stay with an agent for several weeks before continuing the rotation.

When a slot opens up, floaters are hired as official assistants working on a **desk.** Moving from mail hell to assistant hell can take from a few weeks to several months or a year in some cases, depending on turnover and need. As an assistant, the trainee's learning curve takes a steep climb. Not only does she have a bird's-eye view of the whole entertainment-biz spectrum, she also has the ultimate behind-the-scenes entrée and exposure. Thanks to a muting device, with the flick of a switch an assistant can (and is encouraged to) listen in on the nitty-gritty: **sellers** selling scripts and **sign**ing stars, **packaging** pictures and pitching producers, negotiating the dimensions of a celeb's trailer, calming cranky actors after auditions, and dealing with directors demanding their **net profit**s (ha!) or (adjusted) **gross.**

Working for an agent is intense. Grueling. A thirteen-hour day—7 A.M. to 8 P.M.—for dirt pay. To top it off, you are not only an assistant but, for clients, also a travel agent and shrink. Only about one out of ten trainees will make it through the program. Burnout is rampant, and so is a fifteen-pound weight gain! Bound to someone else's every whim, an assistant tends to lose sight of herself. Don't worry, you'll take off the extra weight in six to ten months, when you move on to your new coveted development-assistant job (although you may gain it back when you get a D expense account).

the temp alternative

One way to land an assistant job at CAA, William Morris, ICM, UTA, or any entertainment-assistant job for that matter, is through an L.A. temp agency. A number of companies—Executive Temp, All Star, Friedman, Comar, and Right Connections, to name a few—have contracts with agencies and studios and constantly supply a flow of warm bodies to the biz.

temp warning #1: To be a temp, you've gotta type. Do yourself a favor and learn how. A typing course will serve you better in the biz than any graduate-level film-studies seminar. (Mom, you were so right.)

temp warning #2: Some of these places are a bit of a trip. At Friedman be prepared to be greeted with attitude by employees who don headsets and behave like stressed-out agents brokering Brad Pitt's next multi-million-dollar movie deal—when in fact they're just sending recent college grads to copy scripts for hours on end. At Right Connections you might be equally put off by the proprietor's shrill doggy or the faint canine aroma of the office.

temp warning #3: Temps are often treated terribly, walked over by "real assistants" with permanent jobs, and ignored by everyone else. But being a temp pays and is a way to make some cash while you settle in. And you've got a chance to make contacts, learn, prove yourself, and perhaps (with some luck) even turn a temporary job into a permanent position (which *does* happen).

assistanthood

Ah, assistanthood—the Holy Grail of breaking into the movie business. Why? The only way to get started is at the bottom. There is no school for becoming an executive. The only way to learn **the industry** is to be knee-deep in it. The only way to learn is by example and by osmosis. Assistant jobs in Hollywood are coveted because they are the equivalent of apprenticeships.

All right, so you've hooked yourself up with an assistant job, through an internship, temping, the mailroom, networking, some way, somehow. What should you expect? To a certain degree that depends on the kind of assistant you are. Oh, yes, there are various gradations of Hollywood assistants. Some executives have several assistants, termed First Assistant, Second Assistant, Third Assistant, and so on. These assistants operate in a sort of musical chairs. The eldest assistant (or the one who has been there the longest) is the First Assistant. The greenest of the bunch is the Third (or Fourth or Fifth). When the First Assistant graduates and moves on, the Second

Assistant becomes the First. The First Assistant is in the line of fire. The Third Assistant is a bit more removed from the exec, except, of course, if the Second Assistant is sick and the First Assistant has to run to the bathroom. Then the Third assistant must be there, waiting in the wings, reading to take the reins—or at least the incoming calls.

This assistant-stratification system can also work like this:

creative assistant: Most senior assistant, is involved with tasks on the "creative" end like logging scripts; reading scripts; compiling script notes; executing writer, director, or casting lists; typing pitch memos and response letters to agents.

executive assistant: Number-one secretary and an exec's lifeline. The executive assistant is there for the maven, play by play, minute to minute throughout the day. He or she places all calls for the exec, schedules meetings and appointments (and tells exec where to go and when and how to get there), and makes reservations. The executive assistant's tasks often get personal—appointments with the masseuse and appointments with an agent are fair game. Reservations may have to be procured for lunch with a director or dinner with a husband. Calls must be placed to the pediatrician and the studio head alike.

office assistant: The fire-dog assistant—the one who picks up the pieces, fills in on phones when the executive assistant steps away, and helps the higher-ranking assistants with their tasks. In other words, the office assistant takes directives from the other assistants. Thank God for interns and the occasional temp—even the office assistant has *someone* to boss around.

What kind of assistant you start off as is not important. What is are the qualities you exhibit each day. Here are the top ten:

1. **Attention to detail:** Make lists. Make signs. Make notes. Don't let anyone or anything or any meeting or any script fall through the cracks.

2. **Anticipation**: Always be one step ahead. Figure out what's going to happen next. Your exec is stuck in a meeting and should already be en route to a lunch date with a producer? Call the producer's office. Can he make it at 1:30 P.M. instead? Then call the restaurant. You have cleaned up a mess before it happened and averted drama and trauma (which, by the way, would have been primarily your own because your exec would have burst out of her office flipping out: "Oh my God, so-and-so is waiting for me! Why didn't you do something? Shit, shit, shit!").

3. **Writing right:** Never underestimate the power of the grammatically correct sentence.

Writing well will serve you well. Scribe perfect letters and memos. Proofread and spell-check. Twice. Careless mistakes are moronic mistakes. Avoid them at all costs.

4. **Good attitude:** You know what I'm talking about.

5. **Organization:** No matter how sloppy and all-over-the-place your executive is, no matter how many sticky notes she has plastered all over her desk with fragments of thoughts and things to do, and no matter how impossible it seems, you must make order out of chaos. I promise, your life will be more pleasurable for it.

6. **Memory/recall:** Remember how you crammed for exams not long ago? Use those powers of concentration now to memorize and recall the answers to questions like:

What was that script we saw about the cross-dressers in Iowa?

Who was that red-headed writer who came in for a meeting on a rainy Tuesday in June?

Who directed that movie I liked, you know, the one with Chris Tucker and that cute little girl who lip-syncs to Mariah?

What's the number over at New Line?

If you can file away random information and

dredge it up from time to time, you'll be regarded as alert, eager, and reliable.

7. **Quiet aggression:** Don't walk all over anyone, but don't let anyone walk all over you. Fight for what you need (i.e., what your exec needs)—that lunch reservation, that late FedEx delivery, that missing fax—in the kindest way possible.

8. **Loyalty:** Serve and protect by any means necessary. If you don't have something nice to say about your exec, you know how the saying goes—just shut up. Ill words will only come back to haunt you.

9. **Work ethic:** Be the first to arrive in the A.M. And the last to leave in the P.M. And in between you are there to work. Period.

10. **Common sense:** I can't really help you here. You have it or you don't. If you have it, you're destined to go far.

taking what you can get

Any assistant job, even receptionist, is a legitimate entry-level position. Take what you can get. *Do not* be a job snob. Joel Silver (producer of both the *Die Hard* and *Lethal Weapon* series) started as Lawrence Gordon's (producer of *Boogie Nights* and *48 Hrs.*) driver. This year's intern is next year's creative executive. Your title is not important. Your first job in the industry will not be your last. If need be, lower your expectations. Go work for a company that makes soft-porn B-cable movies and you will still learn plenty. Experience is the name of the game. Just think how sorry you'd be if you were still waiting for Prince Charming or a supermodel (take your pick) to de-flower you. The same applies here. As soon as you know what you're doing, you'll move on.

use me

(.abuse me)

Everything you wanted
to know and were afraid
to ask about Hollywood
hazing.

So I don't know what you've heard about this job, but it's gonna be a lot of work for shit wages. A lot of shit work for shit wages—picking up his dry cleaning, gassing up his car, getting him coffee, getting him lunch, and getting him laid. And he can be, well, difficult at times. . . .

—Outgoing assistant to incoming assistant in
Swimming with Sharks

yes, they stooped that low: things that weren't beneath them

Abuse is an inevitable part of an assistant job in Hollywood. There is a sick cycle of assistant abuse. Like a sorority or fraternity hazing ritual, twisted assistant torture is something the whole club has been through and therefore will put you through, too. Remembering their own assistant years with loathing, they'll do unto others as was done to them—consciously or unconsciously (and in the future you might, too).

But would *you* scrub phlegm out of a breathing tube after a boss's pneumonia bout? Wear a beeper in order to be "on call" at all hours? Clean his house? Trim his beard? Pack and unpack her belongings for a move? Remove a dead mouse from his office? Buy her birth control? Retrieve his fat analysis from an obesity doctor? Go through her garbage in search of a favorite felt-tip pen? Procure the infamous Pamela and Tommy Lee sex tape? Baby-sit his friend's

On the D tip:

If as an assistant you can use your wiles, common sense, patience, and creativity to "produce" your superior's personal life, one day soon you will be qualified to produce a movie.

noisy parakeet? Chauffeur her to a waxing appointment, circling city blocks until her bikini line is bare? Could you figure out a way to get Johnny Carson five hundred pounds of ice delivered to a dock along the Nile or else? Could you locate an antique fourteenth-century crucifix within an hour for a director? Well, D's I know did all these things once upon a time.

"Mon Dieu!" you weep. "Oh, that's nothing," I tell you. Let me go on. Here are some true stories of assistant torture. Names have been changed to protect the innocent and not-so-innocent.

First, a glimpse at the travails of Andrew Assistant:

One day Andrew Assistant's boss (Bastard Boss) complimented him on his tie. "Thank you," said Andrew. "I want one," said Bastard. Andy called the store. "Sold out," they said. "Last season's pattern." "Uh-oh," thought Andrew. He broke the news. "Call Calvin Klein," said Bastard Boss. "Tell *him* who I am." Andy finally reached Calvin— well, not Calvin himself but one of Calvin's corporate-relations reps—who located a tie in Texas.

Cut to: Tuesday, 10 A.M., trailer of Tom Talent: Boss and Assistant arrive decked in twin ties. "Horrible humiliation," bellowed Bastard. "You mock me! I will not be seen on this set wearing the same tie as my assistant! Take it off now."

And Andrew did.

"And never, ever wear it again!"

He didn't (at least not when Bastard was around).

"Someone call Amnesty International!" you cry. "Not before you hear Adele Assistant's woes," I reply.

Fade in:

INT: Malibu—day

A Sunday morning. Adele Assistant is relaxing (sort of; she does have a script in her lap) on the sofa at her parents' beach house. Or she is relaxing until Ballsy Boss calls.

Off camera:

SFX: Phone rings.

Adele: Hello.

Ballsy: Adele, it's Ballsy. Boyfriend and I were going to have a bagel brunch in bed, and I just was going to go out to pick up the cream cheese, and I couldn't remember—do I like Philadelphia Light or Philadelphia Free?

Adele: You like Light.

Ballsy: Are you sure, because the Light has fat, doesn't it?

Adele: I'm sure, because once you said that the Free had a contrary consistency.

Ballsy: Oh, yeah. (Pause) You're out here, right?

Adele: You just called me here.

Ballsy: I know. So, um, will you go pick some up and bring it over to us? And, oh, get some bagels, too—sesame, poppy, and cinnamon raisin.

Adele did.

Ballsy's chutzpah can only be eclipsed by Allen Assistant's boss, incidentally also named Allen, who asked his underling to change his name because there were too many Allens in the office and it was confusing to the elder Allen. As it turned out, Allen's boss also didn't care for his assistant's handwriting and wanted to know if Allen Jr. could alter his signature as well.

Allen agreed to be addressed by last name, but found he could not do much about his penmanship.

Last but not least, here's what Abe Assistant endured when his boss, Bitchola, was detained in the Big Apple and apparently had no clean undies remaining. Suffice it to say that her snazzy hotel had a laundry service. Suffice it to say that she was blocks away from Bloomie's, Bergdorf's, Bendel's, and Barneys. But Bitchola would not think of buying her own bloomers. Instead, from a taxi, she called Abe Assistant across the country, demanding that he phone La Perla lingerie store on Madison and arrange for new, fresh undies to be messengered to the Regency immediately. Then she abruptly "had to jump," leaving Abe to agonize over the size of his boss's ass. He didn't want to offend her by getting underwear too big, but if it was too tight and she was uncomfortable, he would definitely live to regret it. He consulted Avery Assistant, who was Bitchola's Second Assistant. Avery refused to run the risk of involvement. Abe was on his own. He called the store. "Does she prefer thongs?" they asked. Like he would know! He settled on one thong and two briefs the size of which was decided upon by the shop's expert manager, based on his description of Bitchola's petite but rounded buttocks.

By now you may be laughing or cringing or both. You don't believe these stories? Do you really think I could make this shit up? I am aware that these nearly true tales *sound* like scenes from a previously undiscovered Molière farce. We *are* talking comedy of the absurd. Forget "expect the unexpected"—expect the unimaginable.

the value in violation

There *is* something to be garnered from such seemingly nonsensical duties, however. If as an assistant you can use your wiles, common sense, patience, and creativity to "produce" your superior's personal life (solving problems from her pool's heat generator to his car's carburetor, from the case of the late or missing nanny to the caper of the late or missing chicken Caesar salad with dressing on the side, from the double-booked-meeting catastrophe to the over-the-limit-expense-account disaster), you can produce a movie. After all, the producer is a feature's number-one fix-it person: the one who finds a way to deal with the stars' demands, the director's mood swings, and the studio's tantrums—the one whose job is to make life on set run as smoothly as possible.

dealing with what you're dealt

Granted, until you earn your glorified title, screen credit, fee, and profit share, rising above this craziness is not easy, nor is maintaining a saintly façade. In the meantime there must be a measured cognitive dissonance involved. Until the day you get your own assistant, you'd better learn to suppress your inner screw. For now, being smiling, cooperative, thorough, and nice nice nice must be your mission. Such sweetness in the face of sadism requires much discipline. Assistanthood, therefore, weeds out those who are not completely fixated on making it in the movie business. Survivors remember how badly they want to get to where they're going—and are keenly aware that it takes time to get there. Now is the time to pay those dues.

Having "real people" in your life, like parents and friends who have nothing to do with **the business** (and wouldn't *want* to have any part of the business for love or money) can help to keep proper perspective and balance. Realize also that the abuser is a warped person exorcising her or his demons. The abuse is not a reflection on you but rather on his or her own derangement. In fact, it is comforting to convince yourself that the on-the-job you is a separate entity from the actual you. Protect yourself. Shed that bruised skin at the end of each day. Leave the insanity at the office. Visualization also works.

Picture yourself dictating back to your boss. Imagine yourself several years down the road—you are above her, giving him orders, exacting revenge. Too abstract? Small, discreet acts of sabotage can also calm one's nerves. A little saliva in his soup can go a long way (I am told).

the fine art
(of menial tasks)

Suck up. Swallow hard.
Learn to give good
phone and make love to
the Xerox machine.

Gangster Chili Palmer, aka John Travolta:

"I'm going into the movie business, I'm thinking about producing."

"What the fuck do you know about making movies?"

"Well, I don't think a producer has to know much."

—From Barry Sonnenfeld's **Get Shorty**

get over yourself!

Once you walk through the door your first day on the job, who you are and where you come from are utterly irrelevant. You may be a Harvard grad, and your boss may be a college dropout who doesn't know her whos from her whoms. Well, there are plenty of undereducated legends in the entertainment business—Barry Diller (chairman, Home Shopping Network and Universal TV), Jeffrey Katzenberg (founding partner, DreamWorks SKG), Ron Meyer (president, Universal Studios), and David Geffen (founding partner, DreamWorks SKG) are among them. So what if you are smarter, more interesting, more sophisticated, and more articulate than the senior VP? So what if you have three degrees including an MBA and speak four languages? He has business experience under his belt and on his side—and you have lots and lots to learn. First learn to suck it up.

On the D tip:

When morale runs low, try repeating the mantra "This is more fun than making out with Woody Allen."

you and your buddy, the xerox machine

There will be screenplays, articles, letters, memos, **proposal**s, **treatment**s, plays, and an occasional 874-page tome by John Irving. Dealing with the copy room can be downright dismal for a D's assistant.

Repeating the mantra "This is more fun than making out with Woody Allen" is one technique for maintaining a good attitude toward one of the most menial of tasks. On a more serious note, making the most of Xeroxing is very vital. Read whatever it is that you are copying. Think not of "ink on paper" but of imperative information you have the opportunity to absorb. Information is your most valuable commodity. The more you can spit out and regurgitate the better. So if the pile before you is a screenplay, memorize the title, the author, the agent, the agency. Scan the pages for a general sense of plot. I guarantee that this knowledge will be bizarrely useful one day: You will have been promoted, at a different job with a different company, when a new script by the same writer will appear. You will be able to say, "I am already familiar with **Alan Smithee**'s work. I read his spec *Honey, I Shrunk Your Shirt* when I was working over at Coming Attractions, and we passed."

I can't help you to avoid paper cuts, but clearing a paper jam should not raise your blood pressure. Follow the flashing instructions and those inside the copier's orifices, all the while talking to the machine. Naming the Xeroxer initially helps to establish a good rapport for the copying to come. I named my company's machine Suzanne after a third-grade copycat classmate who emulated me more than I could bear.

While copying, watch for page numbers as the paper is spewed out. In some companies assistants and interns must initial the backs of scripts they have Xeroxed. If a page is absent, blame will be properly registered. You never know in whose hands the script will wind up. Always assume your baby is going to the top. Take heed: An assistant was once fired when the screenplay Arnold Schwarzenegger received was missing page sixty-three.

dialing for divas

The phone in Hollywood is not just about simple communication. It represents much, much more, philosophically and practically. Here is an analysis of the supreme merits of The Telephone:

The number of calls received by executives, the number of calls placed by executives, how quickly those calls get **returned,** the number of calls an executive needs to **return,** and the number of their calls that an executive doesn't get returned to them are all true, tangible measures of power in Hollywood. The more important you are, the more calls you receive and the faster the calls you place to powerful people get returned.

Practically speaking, the phone is a place to make and build relationships, to schmooze, to flirt, to work it—this goes for assistants, too. As an assistant you will have the opportunity to talk to the people to whom your boss gets to talk. You will be connecting them to your executive, taking their messages, and delivering messages back. They will get to know your voice, and if you are especially proficient, helpful, and charming—in short, if you give "good phone"—they just might remember *you*.

telephone trafficking

Your success as an assistant is inextricably linked to your telephone skills. The thing is, executives consider their time far too valuable to make telephone calls themselves—which would entail wasting precious moments finding a number, seconds dialing, and (God forbid) a minute leaving a message. Instead the exec expediently goes about **rolling calls,** instructing his assistant, "Get Drew on the line, then I want Wesley, then Dustin, then Brett. The assistant digs up the proper digits (usually she'll have a computerized Rolodex). Punches 'em in.

"Ring."

"Little Girl Lost Films."

Assistant: "Hi, this is me from Mike De Luca's office at New Line. I have Mike on the phone for Drew."

....

Scenario 1:

Drew is in. Drew comes to the phone.

Drew: Mike?

(Notice the savvy assistant waits to get the object of the call on the phone *first*. Who comes to the phone first and who must wait for the other party to come to the phone is very political and touchy. Many exec callers will not pick up the phone until the desired call-ee is already on the line).

Assistant: Hold on, Drew, I'll get him for you.

Assistant either:
- **conference**s *to Mike's phone in his office*
- **patch**es *the call in to his cell phone*
- *transfers the call to him in a conference room*

He is on the line.

Assistant: Go ahead.

Scenario 2:

Drew is not in or not available.

Assistant: Just tell her Mike D. **left word?** Thanks.

....

Incoming calls in need of return or calls placed where a message has been left are notated on the **phone sheet.** This tally of calls must be impeccable. A name or number accidentally dropped could mean a call left in phone purgatory, forever unreturned. Such a call to an important muckety-muck will no doubt come back to haunt a poor assistant.

Now, I'm not gonna kid you. The phone can be very tricky and intimidating at first. Though execs never know how the phone works, assistants are expected to perform complicated procedures perfectly when a boss calls in from a plane or the Cannes Film Festival or the treadmill and demands to be connected here and there with this one and that one.

The technicalities of each telephone system are always different, but the key is always the same: Be Zen. Take a deep breath and remain calm, realizing it is, after all, only a telephone (an instrument you have used since you first began to talk).

Of course, my first day on the job I felt like Lucille Ball on crack. Virtually no one called whom I didn't creatively disconnect—but then again I didn't have the benefit of reading this handy book.

proactive eavesdropping

When placing calls for an executive, it is common practice to stay on the line and listen to the conversation in order to efficiently place the next call when she is finished. Listen carefully to your executive when she is on the phone. Don't type. Don't doodle. Concentrate! If she is in the office and you haven't placed the call, ask her if you can pick up her guest phone or if she will use the speaker phone so that you can listen in while she is negotiating or on a conference call. Hearing her **pass** on a project to agents, giving notes to writers, discussing the details of an **option** with a lawyer, etc., is how you will learn—learn the lingo, learn how to talk the talk, learn what to say and what not to say, learn how a movie gets put together. It is how you will learn to do *her* job one day—and how to **get fucked** as seldom as possible.

phone camps: headsetters versus telephone traditionalists

As an assistant, one of the few choices you will ever have (besides whether to order your tuna sandwich on rye or whole wheat) is whether to use a headset, remote headset, or normal receiver. Each has pros and cons.

Picking up the phone all day every day can do damage. Nasty neck cramps are a Hollywood hazard. The headset, a device that attaches to your phone, eliminates the neck issue but can be a pain to constantly remove as you run into your exec's office, the bathroom, the Xerox room, or to pull coverage, etc.

Although headset wires tend to get tangled in long

locks, headsets can serve the handy dual function of headband (if only they were designed in suede or crushed velvet!). The basic headset comes in several varieties: One fits in and around your ear (this sort of headset has been known to cause calluses and even ear infections). Another headset looks like a Walkman with either double- or single-ear headphones. A remote headset is attached only to your head, so you never have to run for the phone—it's with you wherever you go. But because the remote headset operates like a cell phone beaming into your brain, it can't be so good for you.

With any sort of headset, one tends to resemble that "*Time* and *Life* TV operator standing by." The telephone-operator look is especially abhorrent to guys.

When I eventually settled into the traditional telephone camp, I developed a special antidote for phone-induced neck aches: Remove pillows from bed. Roll up towel lengthwise. Lie down on your back with the towel under your neck and your head back. By morning you should be healed and ready to face a new day of tele-tag.

classified
(secrets for success)

Listen up. Tried-and-true advice, from homework to chutzpah.

(Squeal) Project!

—Cher Horowitz née Alicia Silverstone in
Amy Heckerling's **Clueless**

secret #1: *lie*

No word in the movie business can be believed. Your parents might have taught you that lying would get you in trouble, but they were sooo wrong. Lying—and lying well—is a vital skill to keep you out of trouble in Hollywood.

Chances are, your boss will be a good role model as a liar. From him you will learn how to intelligently, emotionally, convincingly fake having read a script or manuscript, watched a film, or attended a play when you have in fact only skimmed coverage or seen the trailer.

It is also important to lie effectively on behalf of your boss, or for the sake of your executive's ass (and by extension your own). There are times it is necessary to pretend that she is in the office when she is in fact at the hairdresser in order to protect her from superiors. Other times it is necessary to feign that he is "out of the office" or "in a meeting with a writer" or "stepped away" or is "on the set" when he simply does

On the D tip:

The exec who is a little bit country is just as legitimate as the one who is a little bit rock and roll—embrace your taste.

not want to talk to that particular agent, actor, director, writer, producer, and so forth.

This sort of lying requires you as an assistant to have a mental Rolodex of who's who—and an awareness of whom your exec is trying to avoid. Is the caller worthy of interrupting a meeting? If you make the wrong judgment, you could be damned. Also required are acting skills. Assistants must alter the intonation of their voices, to register:

Exasperation: "Oh, God, you *just* missed him!"

Sincerity: "I know he's *dying* to talk to you—he's going to be sooo upset";

Remorse: "I'm *sooo sorry* you guys have been having such trouble connecting. I know he's been meaning to return your call."

Of course, if there were a moment of truth à la *Liar, Liar,* the same conversation might read: "Oh, he's *in,* all right. He's sitting in his office thumbing through *Vanity Fair,* and he doesn't want to talk to you because you just aren't important enough. And by the way, he's not calling you back today, tomorrow, or ever."

The same techniques should be applied to secure reservations at *the* chic new restaurant and tickets to the hottest Broadway show.

An inflated sense of self-importance is epidemic in the entertainment business. Don't tell your boss that his name did not mean enough to get him a table. After all, there is *always* an available table and there is *always* an extra fifth-row-center seat for a VIP. Remember, where there's a will there's a way. It is not what you ask for but *how* you ask for it. Attitude, people! For example, "I'm calling from so-and-so's office at the Walt Disney Company, and he would like to have dinner tonight at your restaurant. You're booked? Oh, God, he's going to kill me, he promised [insert Gwyneth, Winona, Jada, Liv, Cameron, Neve] that's where they'd go...."

The unsaid presumption in the assistant/executive relationship is "Do for me and someday I will repay you [i.e., get you another job!]. Plainly put: If you lie for your executive, she owes you—big time. Lying will advance your career.

secret #2: ingest caffeine

L.A. has the Coffee Bean and Tea Leaf. New York has plenty of Starbucks. Ice blended or frappacino, latte with skim, double espresso, just a plain cup o' joe, or even a Diet Coke, low-cal or no-cal, I don't care.

On both coasts, showbiz types talk fast fast fast and move faster. Making movies is a game. The winner beats everyone to the punch. The hottest script, the hottest star, the hottest restaurant, club, trend, concept—film is new new new. So you've always gotta be the first—the first in the know, the first to get the script, the first to read it, and the first to make an offer. If another offer is made, you have to be the first to match that offer with a better

one. And if it isn't working out, you've gotta move on—
quick. Caffeine is critical to giving you that special edge.

secret #3: read the trades

It is a well-known fact that the rumors in Hollywood are
always true—especially if they are printed in **the trades.**
The industry's trade publications, the magazines *Variety*
and *The Hollywood Reporter* are therefore a morning ritual for anybody who's anybody—and are the savvy assistant's lifeline and lifesaver. They should be studied like a
cheat sheet for a final.

The trades are tools for becoming an ace assistant, prepared for and able to anticipate the day's onslaught. How
else do you know that someone was fired (note: Cancel
your executive's lunch date with the unlucky slob next
week); someone was hired (note: Send flowers from your
executive); a spec script was nabbed by a rival studio (note:
Place your company's "pass" coverage on your executive's
desk to remind him why he wasn't interested in the concept); an indie film was **picked up** for a fortune (note: Add
director to the actual or mental hot list); a movie **open**ed
at number one (note: This week you will be trying to find
a **cross between** *Titanic* and *Halloween H2O*).

By the way, don't be alarmed if at first you have trouble translating the trades. In trade talk, execs don't resign,
they "ankle"; they're not fired, they're "axed"; directors
don't direct, they "helm"; deals aren't made, they're

"inked"; writers are "scribes," actors are "thesps," presidents are "prexie's," top studio execs are "brass," a star's agents and/or managers and publicists are "handlers," a film's premiere is a "preem," and B.O. stands for "box office." You'll catch on soon enough.

secret #4: recognize a good story when you see one

From your analysis of *Variety*'s weekend **theatrical** box-office gross, you know what **audience**s are looking for. But how do you know a good script when you see one? High-school English taught you what makes a "well-told" tale: plot, theme, conflict, characters, blah-blah. The copious screenplay-writing books talk in terms like "the setup," "the spine," the **first, second, and third acts,** "motivation," what's at "stake," the necessity of suspense and of romantic interest, character **arc** and **back story,** story **beats,** yadda, yadda. Read one of these books if you want, but basically it's all common sense. And the thing is, plenty of bad—i.e., *un*original and *un*interesting—stuff does contain all of these requisite elements. Obviously, every script is not a movie. Here are my favorite tests for discerning which ones are:

- As you read a comedy script, keep tabs on whether you giggle out loud. There is a magic number (seven). But five chuckles count, too.

- Is it a fast read? Are you dying to learn what happens next? Do you carry the screenplay with you into the bathroom and kitchen?
- Or is it an excruciatingly slow, snoozy read that has the effect of a lullaby or tranquilizer each time you pick it up?

Sometimes I don't have a definitive feeling about the script upon completion. But if the story stays with me, matters to me, resonates in the coming hours or days, or if I find myself thinking about a character or a line, I recognize that "there is something there."

That intangible "something there" is difficult to define. It is what moves us emotionally, heightens our senses, the way the best films do. Alas, yes, this "something there" is subjective. A script reader in David Hollander's play *The Sun Dialogues* describes his "something there" as a "visceral" quality. And how does he decide whether the material merits such a label? Well, it is "visceral," he says, "if it makes you feel like jerking off."

secret #5: read and watch the classics

Recognizing good writing is as vital as recognizing a good story. Ultimately a movie is always only as good as its script. It is very hard to ruin a wonderfully told story on-screen. But conversely, even the most brilliant director can't save a poorly told story. How do you recognize phenomenal writing? You just do. But reading classic scripts from blockbusters can be a great help.

In addition to your assigned reading, you should take home some "optional" homework. Read all of the famous scripts that you can get your hands on. Movies that have won Oscars. Films that have made hundreds of millions of dollars. Vary the genres: Read classic romantic comedies like *Tootsie, Moonstruck,* and *Annie Hall;* **broad comedies** like *Animal House, Fletch,* and *Beverly Hills Cop;* study dramas such as *Terms of Endearment, Kramer vs. Kramer, The Big Chill, Rain Man,* and *Ordinary People;* and look carefully at suspense flicks, thrillers, and action movies, like *Fatal Attraction, The Usual Suspects, The Fugitive, Die Hard,* and *Speed.*

If you work for a studio or a production company that has made any of these hits, the scripts will probably be on file. Your company may also have a library. Otherwise the scripts can be obtained through the screenwriters' agents (your company should have reference directories or computer software to research authors and their agents) as **samples.** In addition, when a spec ignites a big bidding war and sells for a ransom, take a look at it. Know the marketplace and be aware of what is being bought.

While it is important to get the feel of what films look like on paper, it is paramount to see the great movies. There is no excuse for being ignorant of the history of film, a history that exists within this century and lives on the shelves at your friendly neighborhood video store. You must take a film-studies class in your living room, absorbing cinema's masterpieces, the films that are constantly referred to, the films that inform filmmakers of today. Through your hours with the classics you will begin to glean an understanding of structure, of drama, of how tension evolves, of what's funny, of what's universal; an understanding of what makes a movie work—you will begin to prepare for being an executive who will develop movies that work.

The following is my own REQUIRED SCREENING list of must-see directors and specific films:

Directors: Woody Allen, Robert Altman, Michelangelo Antonioni, Ingmar Bergman, Bernardo Bertolucci, Frank Capra, John Cassavetes, Joel and Ethan Coen, Federico Fellini, John Ford, Alfred Hitchcock, Larry Kasdan, Stanley Kubrick, Akira Kurosawa, David Lean, Sidney Lumet, Louis Malle, Roman Polanski, Jean Renoir, John Sayles, Martin Scorsese, François Truffaut, Billy Wilder

Movies: *Citizen Kane* (1941), *8½* (1963), *Adam's Rib* (1949), **Annie Hall* (1977), **Au Revoir, Les Enfants* (1987), *Blazing Saddles* (1974), *Body Heat* (1981), *Bull Durham* (1988), *Cape Fear* (1991), *Casablanca* (1942), *Chinatown* (1974), **Cinema Paradiso* (1988), *Diner* (1982), *Do the Right Thing* (1989), *Double Indemnity* (1944), *Easy Rider* (1969), *Fanny and Alexander* (1983), *Gone With the Wind* (1939), **House of*

Games (1987), **Kramer vs. Kramer* (1979), *Lawrence of Arabia* (1962), *Mean Streets* (1973), *Miller's Crossing* (1990), **Moonstruck* (1987), *My Life as a Dog* (1985), *One Flew Over the Cuckoo's Nest* (1975), **Ordinary People* (1980), *Raging Bull* (1980), *Seven Beauties* (1975), *Some Like It Hot* (1959), *Star Wars* (1977), *Taxi Driver* (1976), *Terms of Endearment* (1983), *This Is Spinal Tap* (1984), **Tootsie* (1982), *The Four Hundred Blows* (1959), *The Bicycle Thief* (1948), *The Godfather/The Godfather, Part II* (1972, 1974), *The Graduate* (1967), *The In-Laws* (1979), *The Nutty Professor* (1963), **The Out-of-Towners* (1970), *The Usual Suspects* (1996), **When Harry Met Sally* (1989), *Women on the Verge of a Nervous Breakdown* (1988)

secret #6: find a project

Convincing your company to purchase a project that you have discovered is an important career milestone. Although your having brought the project in will *probably* not technically make you a producer and will not entitle you to a percentage of the profits, it will have worth in other ways.

You will immediately become recognized as someone who has a good eye for material, someone who can recognize a good concept. And if you are lucky, you will be

* Hadley's top-ten favorites

put on this project or will be involved in the evolution of the film from paper to the screen.

How do you place a movie in Development that bears your personal stamp? Why, simply adhere to the remaining secrets, #7 through #15.

secret #7: be prepared

As a result of a Hollywood phenomenon called weekend read, every Saturday and Sunday you and your colleagues will bring home mounds of reading—scripts and treatments and articles and coverage. You will sift through the pile, and every once in a while find a diamond in the rough. It is then your mission to "sell" your superiors on the idea at a subsequent **creative meeting**.

Be well prepared to do so by addressing several questions:

- What appeals to you about the story, the dialogue, the characters, the writing?
- What about the material is commercial?
- Who is the audience?
- If it is a book, will screenwriters be lining up to write the film version?
- Will directors be drawn to **the world**?
- Is there a good role to attract a big-name actor or actress? Whom do you envision in the role(s)?
  (So if the project is a new, modern **take** on *The Wiz-*

ard of Oz à la *Twister*—a high-concept natural-disaster family film—who is Dorothy?)

- What other successful movies is your project like? (Come up with a cross between that will help to pin down your vision. For example, if you describe your film as *G.I. Jane* meets *Top Gun*, the executives will know you are talking about an action movie about a female fighter pilot.)
- If the story is **small**, **thin**, or **internal**, how can it be **opened up** for the big screen?

secret #8: be passionate

Use your most important asset—the courage of your convictions. Be gutsy. Be brave. Dare to be you. Trust your instincts. Value your own opinion. Fight for your point of view. This is simply the only way to be a powerful advocate for yourself and the material you love. Exude confidence, and you will get everyone else to listen to you.

secret #9: remember, you have good taste!

The movie business is subjective, unscientific, chaotic. There is no right and wrong. There are no foolproof formulas. If there is one true movie mantra it is this: "Nobody knows anything." Therefore, everyone knows everything. It all comes down to "good taste." A great Development team is comprised of a conglomeration of people with different sorts of good taste—a CE with a taste for sci-fi, an assistant with a taste for high-concept action/adventure, a VP with a taste for broad slapstick comedy, and so forth. After all, chances are the same executive who chooses to make *Virus* isn't the one who makes *Shakespeare in Love*. The exec who is a little bit country is just as legitimate as the one who is a little bit rock and roll. Embrace your taste.

secret #10: be political

When you are a lowly underling and the sole advocate for a project, the job of swaying a bunch of cranky executives can be a tough one. If you find that your superiors aren't always persuaded, try a more political approach. Convince one other person in the company of the project's worth first (preferably someone within the decision-making ranks, but even another assistant might do the trick), and ask that person to back you up in front of the group. A team approach will help to build consensus and transform your solitary plea to a chorus.

secret #11: be tenacious

If you and your project get shot down by your superiors, don't take the rejection to heart. Keep trying, and keep sharing your wonderful ideas. One of these days the sharks are gonna bite.

secret #12: run the other way

Go where everyone else (in the film community) isn't. If they are all reading the same spec or chasing the same book, go to a play. If they're all over the theater scene, you should be at a comedy club. Don't be a lemming. Look for material in uninhabited nooks and crannies.

secret #13: never let 'em see you sweat

In spite of your boldest efforts there will be times when you feel like a fraud. You'll be unsure, insecure, and brimming with self-doubt. You'll think, "Yeah, maybe no one knows anything, but I know nothing." Just do yourself a favor and *act* like you know what you're doing. Believe me, no one will know the difference.

secret #14: don't forget, your age is an asset

Film is one of the few businesses in which your young age is not looked down upon as a liability. In fact, your youth provides you with a natural niche. Play it up! You will be considered most "tapped in" to what the group that goes to the movies most (ages twelve to twenty-nine) wants to see and regarded as the office barometer for what's hip and **edgy**.

secret #15: be nice

To everyone. The twerp from ICM mailroom will soon have the next Cameron Crowe as a client; one of your readers is sure to sell a sought-after spec. You never know where anyone will end up. But wherever they are, they'll remember how you treated them. D's should do unto others . . . You know the rest.

dressing
(to be a d)

This is the movie business we're talking about here. Superficiality is incredibly important. Image. Perception. Youth. Beauty. Style. They are all synonymous with Hollywood. They count. A lot. I know you can't afford an Armani suit (yet), but that doesn't mean you can't look fashionable. Follow me. . . .

Wake up—time to shop.

> —Richard Gere as corporate raider
> Edward Lewis in **Pretty Woman**

garb for girls

I firmly believe in dressing day into night. In other words, wear clothes to work that can take you through the evening—whatever it may hold. You never know when a drinks meeting with a cute young writer will suddenly turn into a date or when at the last minute your boss will give you tickets he can't use to a premiere or a Broadway show. You have to be good to go. Simple, dark clothes (navy, black) are the best bet, as they are slimming and versatile.

On the D tip:

Good things happen to those who dress well.

what every d-girl needs

The most essential component to this wardrobe is a great, seasonless, black jacket in a light wool, stretch nylon, or crepe. Some of my favorites are Club Monaco, Chaiken & Capone, and Theory. It should fit well and make you feel chic.

The requisite staple jacket can be easily mixed with

flattering pants. I prefer pants to skirts for several reasons: 1) Pants and the connotations of "wearing the pants" make a more powerful statement. 2) Skirts appear as though you are "trying too hard." You want to seem as though getting dressed was effortless. After all, you are thinking about the script notes you're working on, not your pantyhose. 3) Comfort is key. You will be sitting at the computer and running back and forth to the fax machine all day. Wearing something that will be riding up or need pulling down or fussing with is just silly.

Every D-Girl should have a designer touch or two in her ensemble. Designer accessories provide status, quality, and fashion. Sure, they're expensive, but they say "I'm worth it." And you are. With the right shades on as you stroll across the lot (worn on top of your head when the sun has gone down), you will look like a baby maven in the making. In addition, an outfit should be finished with an aspirational Prada or Gucci belt. I am an advocate of the designer sunglasses and belts rather than shoes because they are more practical and cost less. Both are timeless, seasonless, durable items to be worn over and over again.

your trademark

It is important to have a personal accent that defines you and projects your unique sensibility. This trademark should be identified with you and no one else in your workplace. It will help to set you apart and to subliminally reinforce the fact that although you are an assistant, you are an individual with a particular point of view and personality. Some examples of trademarks might include: baby barrettes, baby T's, or baby blue nail polish. Whatever it is, keep it simple, but don't leave home without it.

mandatory maintenance

Keep people in your life who can help you to maintain your own special inner and outer glow—from your therapist to the psychic to the manicurist to that hairdresser who does a quick wash-and-dry for a mere twenty-five dollars (I believe that professional blow jobs are the best kind).

accessories of choice

A Filofax is a must-have for every D-Girl. It's where she keeps her appointments with that hot new director and with that fabulous masseuse. It's where she writes down the drinks date with the agent and the real date with the investment banker. Your schedule is hectic so you don't have enough time to be disorganized! Rely on your friend the Filofax to keep your life uncluttered and to keep you a sane dame.

Smart D-Girl On The Go

Glasses: Gucci

Black Jacket: Club Monaco

Cute little T-shirt: XOXO

Belt: Prada

PRADA

Bag: Old Navy

Pants: Theory

and the essential Filofax

Cool Boots: Steve Madden

The look you *don't* want...

d-guys: the dappers versus the hipsters

Let's be honest, guys don't need to have as many clothes or think about them as much as girls. This is not to say what they wear is not just as important. After all, good things happen to those who dress well. Guys just have to get it right (and that for them is always the hard part).

D-Guys must not make the mistake of being either conservatively dapper (think Tom Wolfe) or tragically hip (think SNL's "Sprockets"). The movie business is one in which art meets commerce—both categories should be represented and transcended in style. In other words, you shouldn't look like a rocker and you shouldn't look like a banker.

a suitable suit, a surefire shirt

rule #1: Always dress for the position you want to have. Dress not for who you are but who you want to be. This probably means wearing a suit to work. The thing is, you'll get more props with a suit. You'll look older, more serious, authoritative, confident—like you're prepping for the art of the deal (which, of course, you are). The suit should be of the three-button variety. A light wool is excellent because it is seasonless, works on either coast, drapes well, and wrinkles less. The key to the suit is not too flashy but not too boring, not too stiff but not too trendy.

Your jacket will come off in the office during the day, making the shirt equally important. Plain-front, European-style shirts are more in vogue and look terrifically cool open without a tie, which isn't necessary. Never wear a button-down collar.

You don't need to have racks of outfits, just a few good things. Go for quality. Go for what lasts. If possible, splurge. Barneys Warehouse Sale (a phenomenon in both California and New York) and Century 21 (designer discount store near Wall Street) are terrific sources for beautifully made Italian stuff at cut rates. Banana Republic is the place for well-designed Donna Karan or Calvin Klein knockoffs.

Having advocated the suit, I must make a qualification or two. The business does have an increasingly casual aesthetic, and for a growing number of high-profile execs, worn jeans have become de rigueur. If you find yourself working for an ultracasual guy, a suit isn't a good idea—but nor is holey antique denim. Look neat and together. Wear nice new jeans (by Diesel or Levi's) with a shirt and jacket as described above. The other situation for which to dress down is a meeting with talent—(for example, some scruffy scribe who might be put off by your groovy garb).

accents

I'm not talking about your New Yawk accent. But your choice of accessories can say as much about you as a bad Long Island or Valley twang!

shoes: A loafer—a little chunky but not too chunky—again, if in doubt lean toward the classic. I'm a fan of Kenneth Cole, Patrick Cox, and J. P. Tod's.

watch: If you don't have some fancy Rolex or Tag from graduation, buy a chrome Swiss Army watch—funky and functional at once.

glasses (sun or real): Frames with a vintagey vibe. You can't go wrong with Paul Smith or Oliver Peoples. A designer insignia on the side of shades is a big *no-no* for guys. Too *too!* Spare and simple all the way.

car: Yes—your car is an accessory. So find a ride with flair. Seek out a used conversation piece—a 1970s Mercedes, Porsche, Mustang, Bug, or Caddie (no more expensive than a new Honda), which will be associated with you and you alone.

name: If you aren't blessed with a first name that automatically sets you apart (like Guymon or Mills or

Down D-Guy

Fab Frames:
Paul Smith

Shirt:
Barneys
New York

Jacket:
Banana
Republic

Watch:
Swiss
Army

The look you don't want...

Pants:
Diesel

and cars...
Porsche, Cadillac,
Volkswagen

Loafers:
Kenneth
Cole

Beau—or Hadley, for that matter), you might want to consider a stage name. Not that there is anything wrong with being a Josh, John, or David, but for a long time you will be just another David in a sea of assistants named David populating lots stretching from Pico to Washington. You will be David *who?* When a peon named Doug became "Disco," identifying himself and the Miramax maven on whose behalf he was calling by a single word, he assumed the status of assistant-legend. In no time Disco was boogying to an exec gig in Sony's chairman's wing (complete with seventeen-thousand-dollar hardwood floors).

hair

Come on, cut it, boys. Don't be afraid. You are the master of your mane. Short and neat sends a message of control. Go to a real old-school Italian barber—the kind that uses an actual razor. In L.A. you can find him on Larchmont Avenue and in NYC down in the East Village. For those who need to express their wild urges through their do, a little streak of color in front is all the rage. A highlight gets the stamp of approval so long as it is in the realm of natural (rather than primary) color.

sex
(& the single d-girl & guy)

What you need to
know about whom to
sleep with.

He's weird. He's strange. He's sloppy.
He's a total nightmare for women. I
can't believe I haven't slept with him
yet.

—Janeane Garofalo in **Reality Bites**

no boys allowed: her p.o.v.

screw the rules When I first became an assistant, I spent an evening sipping chamomile tea with a dashing thirty-five-year-old former studio VP turned independent producer. I had met him a month before at a play reading, and he had given me his business card. I called him, and he agreed to meet with me. In this encounter lie several lessons:

There are no "rules" (as in *The Rules*) when it comes to the biz. Older, successful men will be charmed by your interest and will agree to talk to you (whereas it would probably be inconceivable to obtain a meeting with a female producer of the same ilk). There is much to be gained from such a rendezvous: First and foremost, this is a networking session. You will have made a valuable new high-level connection, with someone who will now return your calls and who might be able to help you set up a project or give you or recommend you for a future job. Therefore, be sure to research this guy beforehand. Don't

On the D tip:

It isn't whom you've slept with but whom you haven't slept with that matters.

play dumb damsel. Impress him. If he's an agent, know every writer on his list. If he's a producer, know every movie he's ever been involved with.

ask for advice When you have the opportunity to sit down with a man who can lend you seasoned, objective advice, you should milk him! The most valuable professional advice I have ever received came from the dashing producer described above. Ironically, he told me to focus on "meeting my class." He said that instead of meeting those who are already in power "like him," I should be getting to know people "like me." "The people who are assistants now," he told me, "will be the players later. They will be rising with you." He also was adamant about consciously meeting two new peers a week, one of whom should be a writer or director. "Relationships," he insisted, "are what it is all about—it's how I find writers for projects, got a studio job, produced my first film, and cemented my production deal." His wisdom has already proved sage. Now that I have risen in the ranks, so have the others who were assistants when I was. And as they gain power and take on bigger jobs, we are able to help one other.

don't do it After the dashing producer and I discussed our mutual careers, he looked at me and asked, "So, do you have a personal life?" Our "meeting" in that moment took an ambiguous but not unexpected turn. Social and business life inevitably blur. Accept this and work it, girls, but don't become involved. Remember, you are always in a more powerful stance if a man hasn't seen you naked but wishes he could than if he already has and has nothing more to gain. Your job is to collect people—don't jeopardize tenuous relationships with sex. Use sexual tension as a lure, but be smart about going too far. The entertainment world is a small one on both coasts, and who has been with whom is common knowledge. It is therefore best to flirt within the business but date out of it. Remember, when it comes to the entertainment business, it isn't whom you've slept with but whom you haven't slept with that matters.

is it a meeting or is it a date? Sometimes dating in the business is in fact inevitable—especially if you live in L.A., where you rarely meet a guy who is not in some way connected to the entertainment industry. To say that business and social life intersect in the industry is an understatement. Meetings are often held outside the office and disguised as social events. Drinks in a hotel lobby, invitations to screenings, to the theater, to readings, to parties, or to dinners—all are activities that might qualify as a "meeting," and this meeting very well might be with a very attractive, interesting, and accomplished man.

So how do you tell if it's a meeting or a date or, in the words of celluloid sista Lynda Obst in her book *Hello, He Lied,* "if he's flirting with me to work or working with me to flirt?" The most jaded of D-Ladies would argue that you *can't tell* because *every* meeting in Tinseltown is about one thing: "Are you fuckable?" I know, this seems like an extreme assessment to me, too. The problem is, you can't tell if it's a date in the ordinary way—by who pays—if you are both on expense accounts. You only definitely know it was a date if you wake up at his place (just kidding). Here are some more subtle clues:

- If he insists on picking you up rather than meeting you.
- If he orders more than two drinks.
- If your drinks meeting turns into a dinner.
- If he orders a bottle of wine at dinner.
- If he calls the next day to say how nice it was to meet you, and if he suggests another "meeting" next week. (It is not unusual for the first date to really be a meeting and the second meeting to really be a date.)

dating talent When dating fellow showbiz devotees, it is best to date the talent (i.e., writers, directors, or even actors). The reasons are twofold: 1) It may not be wise to date anyone who could help you to get a job or set up a project or who might be your colleague or superior at some point (this includes your current boss). In other words, any executive types who could screw up a potentially beneficial career move for you in the future. 2) When it comes to dating the talent, you have the ability and resources to do some reference-checking on your conquest before wasting any of your valuable time or adding him to your personal odometer. You will reserve judgment until you have seen his flick, read his script, or heard his pitch—until you have discerned if he indeed does have talent at all! (If only it were so easy to assess last week's entrepreneurial blind date's stocks, how well the lawyer you were introduced to over the weekend argues his cases, or the skill with which that doctor your grandmother wanted you to meet performs rhinoplasty!) Furthermore, when it comes to writers, directors, or actors, you, as a representative of a studio or production company, are perceived to have the power to hire the talent, recommend them to other Development people for projects, or even just generate buzz (ever heard of the Development couch?). Thus, you automatically have the upper hand in the relationship. Oh, how we just love that upper hand!

smoking in the boys' room: his p.o.v.

the gay mafia Some of most powerful people in the industry are gay, among them DreamWorks SKG founder David Geffen. The so-called "gay mafia" is good news if you are a gay guy entering the entertainment business, one in which there is no need to be closeted professionally *(au contraire,* your sexuality can be a boon).* By the same token, if you are a straight guy with

* Many do note that the gay showbiz community as a whole is more on the Q.T. in L.A. and more out in NYC.

homophobic tendencies (shame!), you'd better lose those hang-ups quick—or get out. You can always be an accountant. Finding that an ambiguous perception of their sexual preference is helpful businesswise, some straight boys I know go so far as to consciously flirt in order to deconstruct their heterosexuality and demonstrate their comfort level in meetings with gay execs or agents.

bad boys: notorious and a success A double standard? In Hollywood?! For the bad-boy execs and producers of the land of make-believe, the evening-news discovery of their name scrawled in Heidi Fleiss's black book, an E! exposé on their high-profile romance with a married starlet, coast-to-coast gossip-column coverage of a sexual display in the midst of a party in plain view of guests, mixed with a little coke, a lot of Ecstasy, a harassment suit or two, is often not a cocktail for getting canned but rather a career catapult. Whether the rogue belongs to the generation raised during the reign of the Rat Pack or the Brat Pack, naughty behavior throughout the years has planted the seed of status and the makings of myth. It's all about myth in Movieville, where those worth remembering, from James to River, lived hard and fast. Of course, those who get away with the most, like late legend Don Simpson (*Top Gun*) or living legend Robert Evans (*Rosemary's Baby*) are also indisputably talented.

dating and mating: power babes There has to be some justice in the world. Here it is: Once upon a time, a hazel-eyed, raven-haired, twenty-three-year-old D-Guy was invited back to the home of a much older Power Babe "to see her Oscar." Well, she showed him her treasure—but no golden trophy was involved. And the next day, when our D wanted to send this prestigious producer lady a perfect project, his call was not returned.

For D-Guys, fucking or even flirting with a highly accomplished celluloid sister is generally futile. You'll only be diminished in her eyes, relegated to the cute list. If you want to be taken seriously, seduce her with your smarts.

dating and mating: d-girls As far as dating your contemporaries in the business—i.e., fellow D-Girls or agents—D-Guys will discover a litany of complications:

1. **Gossip and innuendo:** If you date in the biz, the object of your affection will be watching your every move—or else one of her friends will. As previously mentioned, the same D group is on the same social/business rotation of screenings, readings, and gatherings. Therefore, a mutual D will always be present to report where you were and who you were with and

what you were saying and what you were drinking. What can you get away with? Not a hell of a lot.

2. **Loyalty: A D-dilemma:** You and the D-Girl you're dating are in bed. You're reading a **galley,** which happens to be an exclusive, sneaked submission for your company. Do you share the material with her, betraying the source of the slip and risking that she could score the script herself? No! You roll over. "Don't you trust me?" she asks. "What kind of relationship is this if you have a greater allegiance to a random editor than you do to me?" With that, she snatches the story.

3. **Enough is enough:** When the film world is a common thread, there is a tragic temptation to talk about scripts, movies, directors, and specs with your lover. The pressure to be in the know, to have the right opinion of what you've read, a spot-on analysis of what you've seen, and a mental spreadsheet of box-office numbers suddenly extends from office life to private life. Yuck. Enough is enough.

a mattress Because the ins and outs of sex in the movie business are so uncommonly complex for men, it is not surprising that so many guys choose a benign bedmate: the unestablished "model-actress-waitress" (dubbed a "mattress" by Peter Farrelly, co-screenwriter of *Dumb and Dumber* and *Something About Mary*, in his book *The Comedy Writer*). These aspiring stars are considered fair game, since they belong to a different pool than the behind-the-scenes showbiz broads, albeit that according to one experienced exec the pool is a "shallow one." Ouch.

the sequels
(d's you wanna be)

And now for the coming attractions: Introducing Hollywood's next generation—young mogulettes and moguls in the making. Who says the sequel isn't better than the original?

Sequels suck. By definition they're inferior films.

That's a bullshit generalization, many sequels have surpassed their original.

Oh, yeah? Name one.

Aliens . . . *T2* . . . I've got it, *The Godfather, Part II*. . . .

—From Kevin Williamson's **Scream 2**

the formula

How long does it take to get an office with a door, **buck-slip**s, a proper title, and a comfy expense account? How long does it take to get over the assistant hump (and get your own assistant)? Unfortunately there is no formula, no exact time frame. There are only factors.

One of those factors is plain luck.

Once upon a time, not long ago, in the City of Angels, a lowly script reader was laid off. His guilt-ridden boss helped him land a new gig as an assistant at another production company. Well, after thirty days, the new boss was fired, and simultaneously the company's president fell ill. As a result, within a month's time, the former reader inherited a suite of offices, an executive title, and his own assistant—not to mention a position he could virtually invent.

On the D tip:

Keep showing up, and success is bound to find you.

At approximately the same moment, a gal on the isle of Manhattan was in the right place at the right time. Night was falling, and the aftermath of the Puerto Rican Day parade meant that Fifth Avenue was blocked off. Cabs were nowhere in sight, and she had to get to the West Side. An older man next to her on the corner of Seventy-fifth Street was in the same predicament, and the two commiserated as New Yorkers will on bleak occasions. He offered to walk through the park with her, warning first that if they were mugged, he would bolt. She said fine. He introduced himself and started to tell her that he happened to be a prestigious and prolific producer. She began rattling off his credits. He was impressed. She got her dream job *and* made it safely to Central Park West.

Another factor in upward career creeping is called tenacity.

On a film set far, far away, a highly worshipped Oscar-winning actress pulled a D-Girl assistant aside after the latter was chewed out by her producer boss. The actress told the D-Girl, who felt so unworthy, that her own success in Hollywood was achieved in large part because she simply "kept showing up." Our D-Girl did not quit and at that moment understood the power of sheer perseverance. Incidentally, she is no longer an assistant.

Tenacity also paid off for a certain D-Guy who, many moons ago, was hired by a manic, mangy, messy mogul as his seventh assistant in a calendar year. That year was only five weeks old. Apparently some of the predecessors had left during lunch, and others had gone to the loo never to return. None lasted for more than three days. The mogul resembled Charlie Brown's pal Pigpen each morning upon arrival: As he crashed into the office caked with remnants of oatmeal, memos, faxes, scripts, messages, and mayhem swirled in his wake. D-Guy would not be mentally mangled by the mania. By March he had memorized 462 phone numbers. May marked a record for mogul-assistant longevity. News reached the far corners of the lot. At the commissary, mavens and maintenance men alike nodded reverently. Now he's almost a mogul in his own right.

career timelines

Okay, enough with anonymity. Some real-life young turks are ready to offer their particular paths for your dissection. How did luck, timing, and persistence play a part in their successes? You be the judge. Here are the journeys of seven D's.

Julie Plec, Age 26
VP, Production and Development, Outer Banks

June 1994: Graduates from Northwestern University.
September 1994: Moves to L.A. And begins working as assistant to agent Susan Smith.
March 1995: Takes job as assistant to Wes Craven (*Nightmare on Elm Street*).
March 1997: Is promoted to director of Development, Wes Craven Films.
April 1998: Leaves Wes for Outer Banks to work for writer/producer Kevin Williamson (*Scream, Dawson's Creek*) as his VP of Development and production.

Eric Handler, *Age 27*
Creative Executive, DreamWorks, L.A.

1993: Graduates from UCLA.
1993–1994: Works as assistant to writer/director John Herzfeld (*2 Days in the Valley*) on TV movies and mini-series such as one of the Amy Fisher flicks.
1995: Works as assistant (one of several assistants) to producer Scott Rudin.
Fall 1996: Works as assistant (one of several) to Bob Cooper, president of HBO.
Summer 1996: Follows Bob Cooper to Tristar Pictures. Is promoted to executive assistant (i.e., assistant chief of staff).
Fall 1997: Again leaves with Bob Cooper to his new production-prez post at DreamWorks. Now Eric is a creative assistant (i.e., deals with administration relating to projects, not the personal stuff).
Summer 1998: Eric is promoted to creative executive.

Carrie Richman, *Age 29*
VP, Columbia Pictures, L.A.

1991: Graduates from Harvard.
Fall 1991–Summer 1993: Works as assistant to playwright Wendy. Wasserstein, assistant at Made in the USA, nonprofit production company, reader for Second Stage Theater (NYC).
Fall 1993: Moves to L.A. As assistant, Castle Rock Entertainment.

December 1994–June 1995: Becomes assistant at Columbia Pictures (L.A.).
June 95: Is promoted to creative executive.
January 1998: Is promoted to VP.

Geoff Suddleson, *Age 26*
Director of Development, Universal Pictures, L.A.

1994: Graduates from UCLA
Summer 1994–Winter 1995: Works as assistant to producer/director on set of third *Die Hard* sequel.
March 1995–February 1996: Becomes assistant to director of Development at Tristar Pictures.
February 1996–July 1996: Works as administrative assistant to Marc Platt, president of Tristar.
September 1996: Moves with Marc Platt to his new Universal presidential post, again as his administrative assistant.
November 1996–May 1998: Becomes creative assistant to Marc Platt.
May 1998: Is promoted to director of Development.

Jim Powers, *Age 25*
Director of Development, The Shooting Gallery, NYC

January 1994: Starts as student intern to Larry Meistrich, company founder.
September 1994: Becomes student intern/reader (full-time while attending NYU).

Spring 1995: Is promoted to director of Development.
Winter 1995: Graduates from NYU.

Patrik-Ian Polk, *Age 26*
Director of Development, Edmonds Entertainment, L.A.

1992: Graduates from Brandeis University.
Fall 1992–Spring 1994: Attends and graduates from USC Film School (studies production, writing, and directing).
Spring 1994–1995: Becomes production assistant on *SeaQuest*, NBC Amblin Entertainment show (lands job thanks to Executive Temps agency).
May 1995–April 1997: Becomes story editor, MTV Films, L.A. (again lands job thanks to Executive Temps agency).
April 1997: Hired by Edmonds Entertainment (*Soul Food*) as creative executive.
November 1997: Learns that Edmonds Entertainment will develop *Punks,* a script Patrik has written (and will direct!). Patrik will produce with Tracey Edmonds, and Kenny "Babyface" Edmonds will exec-produce.
July 1998: Is promoted to director of Development.

Tracy Falco, *Age 28*
Director of Development, Spanky Pictures, NYC

Fall 1992: Graduates from Arizona State.
December 1992: Moves to L.A.
January 1993: Works as assistant at CAA to

power agent/company president Richard Lovett.

August 1996: Leaves CAA.

September 1996: Moves to NYC to begin Spanky Pictures post.

September 1998: Receives credit as associate producer of the film *Rounders* (Spanky/Miramax).

a day in the life of a d-girl

You've met my friends—now meet me, Development Girl herself. I live in a studio apartment on the Upper East Side. My building was the one in *The Jeffersons*. You know, the TV show. Movin' on up. I went to Penn, as in the University of Pennsylvania, as in Ivy League, as in not Penn State. Please. Not that anyone in this business knows the difference. That was six years ago.

Now I work for The Studio. Well, actually the Studio Head. Whom, by the way, I've never met. Hell, I've never even laid eyes on him. My object is to get movie material, then get his attention, then get his approval, and of course then get his elusive green light—a signal that remains to be seen in my tenure. Maybe he's color-blind. But that's another story. Here's my story, or at least a look at a day in my life:

· ·

6:45 A.M.: Power jam with Jimmy K., who turns my tummy and tushy tight. I know, you're thinking, "But aerobics isn't trendy anymore!" Hey, cut me a little slack, Madonna aside, no one got skinny doing yoga.

7:56 A.M.: Shower. I have a brain wave. When you have a brain wave, you simply must at that instant run out all sudsy to leave a voice mail for yourself: "Hi, me, it's me, call Craig to request that *Men Busters* spec today."

8:17 A.M.: Throw on a khaki (it is the new black, you know) getup with super-wedgy slides to give me those all-important extra inches. Toss makeup into my bag.

8:33 A.M.: Elevator: Oops. Forgot last night's manuscript, *Slash for Cash.*

8:38 A.M.: Apartment: Retrieve manuscript, but can't find keys.

8:55 A.M.: I left them in the door.

9:11 A.M.: Subway. Try (in vain) not to touch the pole.

9:34 A.M.: Arrive Fifty-seventh and Seventh. Hope and pray no one gets in the elevator with me. Score! Express ride to the fifty-sixth floor. The tippy-top.

9:37 A.M.: Office kitchen. OOoooo! *How* I want that chocolate-chip muffin! Must talk myself down. Grab banana instead.

9:40 A.M.: My adorable intern, Adrienne, is already ensconced in her cubicle. Send her out for tall iced latte with skimmed half-caf, half-decaf, two Nutrasweets.

9:41 A.M.: My office. A room of my own—and a room with a view. Times Square, the Empire State, the Hudson—and my own door.

Call Jane to find out if she read *Slash for Cash* last night. She did. We were equally repulsed. She has pass coverage—she'll fax it over.

9:56 A.M.: Adorable intern returns with my caffeine concoction.

Intern: I have Renee on the line.

Renee and I track books.

Me: Have you heard when they're **going out with** the new Richard Ford?

Renee: I think it's **been seen.** It was around last month. At least a **partial** was. Do you know anything about this *Men Busters* spec?

Me: Yeah, it's **out on submission** and it's on my desk. We've been assigned a **territory.** The letter reads "You've got it for Touchstone—**Dictated but not read.**"

Renee: Will you make a copy for me when it comes in?

Me: Sure, but it'll be a **no talk no trade.**

Renee: No problem. Also there's this old Jaws-with-Paws project that was **shelved** at Paramount, and I heard it might be in **turnaround.** And I think the new Jennifer Egan might slip out today.

Me: Who **reps** her again?

Lickety-split hang up with Renee and call Jenny E.'s lit agent:

Me: It's me for Jay. Is he available? Jay, honeybunch, how aaarrre you? Listen, is Jenny E.'s new book in at Double-day, because you know how I worship her and we simply *must* take a look at it.

J: Sweetheart, that book is so not ready. Don't believe the hype.

10:21 A.M.: Meet with boss. Discuss the date she took home last night and the manuscript I took home.

11:31 A.M.: Start casting list. Male lead possibilities for pop thriller project: Think *The Firm* meets *Friends*. Here's who you put on casting lists: all the boys you'd like to date: Ben A., Ethan H., Matt D., and Leo, Leo Leo.

12:30 P.M.: L.A. creative-meeting conference call over the **space fone:**

Blah blah blah blah blah projects and script notes and yadda yadda yadda.

Here's what you do during a conference call with the West Coast:

Read the trades.

Read the *New York Times*.

Pass notes to your colleagues.

1:16 P.M.: Get coverage of *Slash for Cash*, which reaffirms my pass position.

I must call to pass. Ooooooo how I hate to pass. (Making a pass is also not in my repertoire.)

Dial UTA.

Me: Howie Sanders's office, please.

Transferred.

Me: Hi, it's me for Howie. I'm calling about *Slash for Cash*.

Assistant: Are you passing?

Me: Yup.

Assistant: I'll tell him.

Yippeee. Easy.

Intern: I have the Cat's Meow on the phone for you.

*Here's the 411 on the Cat's Meow, a so-cute Jewish homeboy director who asked me to accompany him to his NYC premiere tonight. By the way, The Studio is also trying to **get into bed with** him.*

Cat's meow: I have to cancel. Girlfriend surprised me by flying in. But you're on plus one.

Okay, so here's the thing of it. I knew about the girlfriend situation. The Clearasil girl. I wasn't gonna let her stop me! Now I must absolutely find a drop-dead date by day's end. Drama.

1:30 P.M.: Late for **meet-and-greet** lunch. Dash down Fifty-seventh to Madison straight to Barneys basement. The bad news: Screenwriter Tony is waiting. The good news: He is beyond cute, with a tattoo on his forearm. Here's what you must do when you are *en retard.* Apologize profusely: "Darling, I am soooooo sorry. Can I make it up to you by taking you to the premiere tonight?" More bad news: He is already going to the premiere.

3:39 P.M.: Quicky with Hansen (she's my hair-dresser, not one of those brothers). With my intern, over the dryer's din, I patch and roll and conference and transfer from East Coast to West and back again.

4:39 P.M.: Power-walk to office for meeting with a British playwright with an offbeat off-Broadway hit.

5:14 P.M.: The Brit arrives, and you see, I sort of have a thing for accents. So we discuss his current and future projects, and I casually mention our ample **discretionary fund** for *passionate* purchases as I cross and uncross my legs like Sharon Stone in *Basic Instinct.* Of course I'm wearing pants, so I'm not sure it has the same effect. The Brit is more excited about the fifty-sixth floor. He has never seen the city from such a height. We stroll around the office. He gazes out at Central Park. I pop the question. He would be d-lighted. Hallelujah and phew.

6:32 P.M.: We split for the screening.

7:13 P.M.: Here's who's at the premiere: Penny, Puffy, Marky (Mark). Here's who's missing: Ben, Ethan, Matt, and Leo.

Here's who is not *all that*: the Clearasil girl.

advice

(from those who've arrived)

Some have learned a
thing or two as they've
traveled, tumbled, or
trotted down the Yellow
Brick Road to Hollywood
fortune. Now learn a few
things from them.

We're only interested in one thing:
Can you tell a story . . . can you make
us laugh, can you make us cry, can you
make us wanna break out in joyous
song?

—"Jack Lipnick," head of the fictitious Capital Pictures
in the Coen Brothers' **Barton Fink**

These producers, executives, directors, and celebrities are ready to share some sage advice they'd give to a Hollywood newcomer trying to make it—and the best advice bestowed on them when they were Hollywood virgins.

John Lovitz
Actor, Producer (Big)
Master Thespian/Disney

John admits: "I was a 'Hollywood virgin' from Encino once upon a time! Here's my advice to those Hollywood virgins: Get out of your own way. No doesn't mean no in this business—so don't accept no. Just do it.

"The best advice I ever got was from my manager, Bernie Brillstein. He said, 'Don't look to your left or your right. Don't look at what the people around you are doing. Just look ahead. Figure out where you want to go and go there.'"

Brett Ratner
Director/Producer (Rush Hour)
Rat Entertainment/New Line Cinema

Brett's secret: "It's all about persistence. Never quit. Never be afraid to fail. Think to yourself, 'If I fail, my mom will still love me, my true friends will still be friends, so I've got nothing to lose.'

"Russell Simmons *[Def Jam]* gave me great advice. He said, 'Always go with your instincts and you'll make the right decisions, because your instincts never lie.' I've applied that to the projects I've chosen, my studio deal, the agency I went with. I always think of that advice."

Russell Simmons
Producer (The Nutty Professor)
Def Films

Russell gets real: "My advice to someone starting off in this business is a warning: There is no business more full of shit! The sad reality is that even if you are talented, there is no business more concerned with *making* a product than with the *quality* of that product. Producers may say their job is all about development and getting the script right and getting the story right—which it should be—but ultimately I've found them most interested in just getting the movie made.

"The best advice I was ever given was from Joel Silver. He basically summed up the movie business as 'hurry up and wait.' What he meant was, whether you're a producer or a director or an actor, you always have to be on top of things and act quickly and make the initial decisions in a minute and then be ready for the most tedious, drawn-out process. It all becomes a big waiting game. It takes *forever*."

Aleen Keshishian
Agent, ICM

Aleen's advice: "The entertainment business is like a house. There are many ways in. Usually, however, your first job will not fully utilize your strengths and abilities. We've all made coffee, emptied garbage cans, and answered phones.

"Each morning in my office at ICM, we receive four newspapers and three trade publications *(The Hollywood Reporter, Daily Variety,* and *Daily Variety Gotham)*. We also get virtually every weekly and monthly magazine. We are bombarded by information. My assistant and interns read everything before I even get to the office and help to bring the latest films, plays, and talent to my attention. They also read several scripts each week. They are not just secretaries but bring a lot to the table.

"As a member of the committee that selects trainees at ICM, I look for someone who has a proactive nature, an independent spirit, and a passion for the business. At the same time, I look for someone who is willing to work exceptionally hard for a while before seeing any reward.

"I received really useful advice on my first day as an agent (previously I had been a casting director) from a **manager** who took me out to lunch. He warned me that in a big corporation it is easier to wait for others to voice an opinion; it is easier to operate out of fear. He told me not to be afraid to go out on a limb and to trust my taste and instincts. When I signed clients who were unproven in the industry, like Natalie Portman, I did go out on a limb. I had to say, 'I believe in this person.' Once you are proven right, of course, it is easier the next time around—you have earned the trust of your colleagues."

David Brown
Producer (Jaws)
The Manhattan Project

David warns: "The best advice I could give someone who wishes to be a producer is, don't even think about producing if you aren't ready to face constant rejection. And don't even think about producing if you aren't ready to back your personal and artistic convictions with patience and with fortitude. A producer lives entirely on hope—or, in the words of Arthur Miller, on 'a shoeshine and a smile' (plus talent of course!).

"The most important role of the producer is the ability to identify material for the screen and sell the idea of adapting that material to a financier or a studio, to a screenwriter, to a director, and to actors. The second most important role of a producer is the ability to organize creative talent into a cohesive whole. That is to say, various skills must be meshed in the creation of a movie.

"The best advice I ever received was from Darryl F. Zanuck [founder of 20th Century–Fox], one of the first moguls and the man who brought me to Hollywood. He taught me, to quote Shakespeare, 'The play's the thing.' Nothing counts as much as the story, because it is the story that will attract the director, the actors, the studio, the money. The story is the thing."

Liev Schreiber
Actor (Scream 2)

Liev recommends: "In a little play I did called *Hamlet,* Polonius says to his son Laertes, 'to thine own self be true.' That's the best advice I could give to anyone going into the film business. There are so many models, forms, ideas, opinions, opportunities. The temptation is to become a contortionist in trying to be a success. But the reality is that the only thing of value you have to offer the film industry is *you.* If you aren't in touch with yourself and you aren't doing something that is meaningful to you, it's not going to matter to anyone else.

"Too often people in the movie business see something that works and they want to mimic it, re-create it. Paul Newman gave me great advice. He said, 'If you've done it before, why do it again?' The point is, Don't be derivative. Whether you're acting or producing or directing, you have to reinvent your work all of the time. And if you do, you will keep yourself entertained and therefore keep an audience entertained."

Ruth Vitale

Executive
Co-President, Paramount Classics

Ruth suggests: "The movie business is not just about telling stories. At the end of the day it's about commerce; that's where the focus is. The movie [emphasis on] *business*. Behind every film project is a legion of bankers and lawyers expending enormous energy and effort. Sometimes I wish I'd gotten a JD/MBA degree. That would be a great thing to have, because you need to grasp each aspect of putting a deal together and to understand the ramifications of each minute element.

"My old boss at The Movie Channel once said to me, 'You're only as popular as your checkbook.' That has reverberated. You find out who your real friends are when you are between jobs—when you aren't a buyer."

Barry Josephson

Producer (The Wild Wild West)
Sonnenfeld-Josephson/Disney

Barry is bold: "Be willing to do *anything* that the job requires.

"Focus on the work—that's the best advice anyone could give. Producer Suzanne Todd [*Austin Powers*] told me that. Ultimately it's about the work."

Robert Cooper

Head of Production and Development, Feature Division,
DreamWorks SKG

Bob reflects: "Figure out a way to make your weakness, or what you perceive to be your weakness, a strength. If you feel like an outsider, if you feel ignorant, if you feel unconnected, turn those 'weaknesses' around to make them assets. Those feelings can give you an edge and a fresh point of view in a business where everyone is always looking for that new idea.

"I never got any advice. I really wish I had! But it was just sink or swim for me."

Benny Medina

Manager, Producer (Above the Rim)
Handprint Entertainment

Benny's best: "If you decide to go into the movie business, understand that it is way beyond a full-time job. You have to make making movies your wife, your mistress—your consuming, absolute passion. In truth, through faith and total stick-to-itiveness the extremely talented can do well in this business, the moderately talented can do okay, and the untalented can still do *something!*

"The best advice for me was the absence of any advice. I'm afraid if anyone *had* told me of the perils, the challenges, the obstacles, the risks, of producing, I would have considered it an impossible task."

Doug Liman
Director (Swingers, Go)

Doug counsels: "The most pragmatic advice I could give to anyone who wants to be in the film business is to stop talking about wanting to make movies and go make one. Go produce. Go direct. Whatever you want to do, just do it. If you wait for the right opportunity or for someone to hand you a lot of money, you'll be waiting forever. You might be waiting the rest of your life. But with the right attitude you can literally will a movie into being.

"I was lucky in a sense, because I always knew that I wanted to be in film, always knew exactly what I wanted to do. Then I got to L.A., and it was a lot tougher than I ever thought it would be. I was at an all-time low. I was questioning everything—questioning my very existence on the planet. At that point a mother of a friend of mine made me look at my struggle in a different way, which changed everything for me. She said, 'No matter how hard what you're going through is, your life will never be as exciting as it is right now.' Her advice was about appreciating the struggle, the process. She predicted that someday soon I'd be a 'fancy director' and I'd look back on this moment when my *whole life* was up for grabs. She was right—and that was only a couple of years ago!"

Vivica A. Fox
Actress (Why Do Fools Fall in Love)

Vivica's wisdom: "The best advice I'd give to someone breaking in is to be prepared for more rejection than acceptance—no matter what it is you're doing. But don't ever stop believing in yourself—your time will come.

"I was once told that 'your life can change in a day in this business, so stay focused and positive.' It was true. My life did change in a day—*Independence Day*."

David Seltzer
Manager, *Producer*
Co-President, Industry Entertainment

David's advice "is to work somewhere where you meet a lot of people quickly—young people your age who you can grow up with in the industry.

"The best advice I've received was from my client, Jack Lemmon. A long time ago, when I was graduating from Harvard, he explained to me that you have to start at the bottom and work your way up. He got me my first job as a gofer on a movie set. Let me tell you, it was starting at the bottom—I was walking the script super- visor's dog and taking out the garbage. Jack also told me there are no guarantees in this business for anyone—no matter how talented or smart you are. That has always stuck out in my mind."

Mills Goodloe
Producer (Lethal Weapon 4)
Donner/Shuler-Donner Productions

Mills muses: "Don't be lazy. Think about what you need to do every day before you get to the office. Always be proactive, not reactive.

"Joel Silver *[Die Hard]* told me, 'There's activity and there's action. Any exec in town can do activity—do lunch, make calls, read scripts, schmooze. But at the end of the day, if there is no action, all of that activity is meaningless.' I think this is great advice. Be a person of action. For example, I'd rather have an exec working for me who did nothing all day but could then spend twenty minutes on the phone at six P.M. closing a deal or hiring a writer."

Allison Segan
Producer (Saving Private Ryan)
Furthur Films

Allison's answer: "I tell people, if you can find any other way to make a living, do it. There are at least five million other things you can do for work in this world. The film business is *not* like winning the lottery. The only people who should be in film are the people who truly *love* film.

"After I graduated from college, my mother gave me great advice. She told me to go out to California (to 'get it out of my system!'), and she told me not to be afraid to fail. I think that taking a chance, taking a risk, and putting yourself in a position where you *might* fail is important—so many people never do."

Stefan Simchowitz
Producer (House of Yes)
Bandeira Entertainment/DreamWorks SKG

Stefan's philosophy: "Find out in your heart what you truly want, what truly turns you on about the business—whether it's to create, whether it's the fame, the money, the thrill of entrepreneurship or the love of film. Be honest with yourself and follow your path accordingly.

"Herb Allen [entertainment investment banker guru and former chair of Columbia Pictures] told me, 'For the first ten years of your career in the business keep your eyes and ears open and your mouth shut.'"

Carla Hacken
Executive
Senior Vice President, Fox 2000

Carla's call: "My advice to an aspiring executive is don't worry about having a high profile—let your work speak for itself.

"And the best advice I've gotten was from another executive: 'Never be afraid to have an opinion.' "

Jack Leshner
Executive
Senior Vice President, Miramax Films

Jack explains: "There are two film industries. They are intertwining; they live and work side by side. But ultimately they are separate, one cares about the work. One cares about everything else: the money, power, sex, status, games—you name it. Decide which you want to work in and seek out that industry. I've been at companies where I've been able to be about the work (not that I don't have to deal with the people who are about the money and the power). My advice is to figure out: Are movies your means or are movies your end?

"Stephen Woolley, producer of *The Crying Game*, gave me great advice. At the time I was living in London. I had a great job making interesting movies, and I had just received a job offer back home. He said to me, 'Do you want to be an expatriate?' His question crystallized everything. I knew that sooner or later I wanted to go back to New York. 'If it is sooner or later,' he told me 'go now.' People waste time in their careers, doing things they don't care about, things that aren't getting them where they want to go or, in my case, living somewhere they don't ultimately want to be. If you want to run a studio someday and you are living in New York City working in indies, move to the West Coast now, or vice versa. It is never an easier time to go than at this moment. The best time is now."

Guymon Casady
Executive
Senior Vice President, Propaganda Films

Guymon says: "Don't jump around from job to job to get a better title or a little more money. Instead position yourself somewhere where there is clearly some stability, some future, some sort of longevity. You've got to figure out how to survive in this business. You can't think in terms of short-term gains.

"Tom Strickler (Endeavor Agency) told me when I was starting out to get myself into 'a high-traffic situation'— someplace that was making a ton of movies, someplace where I'd be coming into contact with hundreds of people. He said 'opportunities come when you maximize your exposure.' I still think that's great advice."

Brad Wyman
Manager, Producer (Trees Lounge)

According to Brad: "You have to have the same energy and persistence as everyone else. In part that drive comes from loving what you do. I don't realize how hard I'm working because for me film is a disease, a religion. I learned more about Christmas from Frank Capra than from my family.

"The best advice about producing motion pictures was told to me by Elliott Kastner *[Angel Heart]*. He says,

'Rule 1: Get the money.
Rule 2: Never forget to get the money.
Rule 3: Always remember to never forget
      to get the money.'"

Francine LeFrak

Producer (Mi Vida Loca)
LeFrak Productions

Francine's facts: "Here's my advice: If you are looking for a friend in show business, buy a dog! Know that the people you work with are not your family and they are not your friends. People get intoxicated by business relationships and confuse them with personal relationships—and wind up getting hurt.

"I was once telling the producer Larry Gordon *[Field of Dreams]* a Hollywood someone-told-someone-something story, when he picked up a little plaque which he keeps by the phone. He slid the sign in front of me, turning it around for me to read. It's imprinted with great advice: CONSIDER THE SOURCE. Meaning, if you look for and understand the *motivation* behind what you hear, much about this business will suddenly become clear."

Jason Blum
Executive
*Senior Vice President, **Acquisitions** and Co-Production,*
Miramax Films

Jason's words: "This is my advice: Learn how to sell. The
movie business is all about sales—whether you're selling
an actor on a part, a director on a script, or a studio on
a movie. As an acquisitions exec I am technically a
'buyer,' but ironically the most important part of my job
is selling. I have to sell a distribution plan or I have to
sell Miramax as a company to the person I am buying
the film from, and I then have to sell or pitch that film
to Miramax to convince them to buy.

"To sell you have to first of all have something you believe in, and then you need a lot of confidence and
tenacity. I actually learned how to pitch, and how to
close a deal, by renting apartments as a real-estate
agent and selling cable door to door, which I did while
trying to break into the business. After a while I got
pretty good at selling that cable—when I started, I
would only sell to about one in ten people who answered the door. By the time I finished, I was selling to
about one in three. I'm actually not sure if I'd be as successful at what I do now without the experience of
those sales jobs—they were really invaluable.

"The best advice I've been given is life advice, really,
from a philosophy professor/mentor, Mr. McCarthy, in

college. In essence it's simple: 'Don't take a single day for granted.' I try to apply that message to my work. In terms of the movie business it means learning to sort of 'part the seas'—prioritizing, not jamming every day full of fifty gazillion cell-phone calls, meetings, and screenings that might not get you anywhere. Those calls definitely don't count if you're talking to the wrong person on the phone. And those meetings mean little if, at a film festival of a thousand people you're bothering with the nine hundred and eighty-five who *aren't* doing deals rather than the fifteen who *are*."

Susan Cartsonis
Executive
President, Wind Dancer Films

Susan is specific:

"1. Take the worst job at the best place. Go to a place you can learn from the best and make yourself indispensable.
2. Do *your* job perfectly first, then find a need and fill it—expanding the parameters of your job until you move up a level.
3. Choose mentors and let them know they've been chosen. There's nothing more flattering than being told you are a role model. Choosing a mentor is a prime way to insinuate yourself into someone's good graces. Once you have a

mentor—real or imagined—observe carefully and learn as much from their mistakes as you do from their successes.

4. Be fun and seemingly ego-free. Make yourself a pleasant presence who everyone is happy to have around. Without becoming Eve Harrington, find ways to create an aura of fun and helpfulness around you. What you wear, the jokes and stories you tell, the cappuccinos you fetch and the way you deliver them—all serve to define you as a person who can work with talent and rise to the next level.

5. Look at every task as an opportunity to prove yourself, and do it perfectly—from Xeroxing a manuscript to meticulously answering phones to writing coverage. Let no task be too small for your attention, and follow through on *everything*.

"The best advice I ever received was from producer Sara Colleton—back when she was senior VP of Fox and *my* mentor. It was about being political in order to protect your job. She taught me to do your job as though you don't care if you lose it. If you operate out of fear, you will be ineffective. If you are fearless (or at least pretend to be), you will succeed."

afterword

Musings on the media
migration of a generation.

generation e!

Hollywood hysteria is not a recent phenomenon. Movies and movie stars have, of course, always captured our imaginations and attention. There *is* something different, however, about the *Entertainment Weekly* or *Premiere* magazines you pick up at the supermarket checkout line and something different about tuning in to E!, *Access Hollywood, ET, Extra, Show Biz Today,* or *Rough Cut* (can they come up with any more of these shows?!) on the tube. There is something different about *the way* the popular media cover entertainment: The subject of all of this "news" is not just the movie stars—rather it is the *business* of making movies.

I know, it's hardly a revelation: The public is fascinated with the movie business. I mean, who can't quote weekend box-office grosses? And if you can't, where have you been? After all, these days blockbusters land on the cover of *Time* and *Newsweek.* (The week of July 4, 1996, *Independence Day* made both covers simultaneously: "Aliens have Landed" on *Time* and "Out There" on *Newsweek.*) On top of that, mavens—Michael (Eisner), Steven (Spielberg), and Ted (Turner)—are household names. We know Michael Ovitz's Disney severance and Michael Eisner's salary.

No surprise. We all live in a media-savvy—cross that out—media-*obsessed* culture. But professionally, my generation is particularly enchanted with the entertainment business. We realize full well that entertainment is America's number-one export ("as if"!). We are attracted to the international influence of the medium. We are compelled by the power of the people responsible for bringing it to the United States and the world. We are drawn because of an insatiable global marketplace. We are sucked in by the excessive media coverage, the megabucks, the allure, the pretty people, the cachet, the perceived glory, the glamour, the recognition, and the lifestyle.

In its May 1998 article about young Hollywood, "Moving in the Fast Lane," *Newsweek* declared, "After several years of floundering around in slackerville, young people have found a new place where they can work hard, get rich and party like it's 1999." Think Jeff Spicoli meets Gordon Gekko. *Variety* on July 16, 1998, reported that some thirty film and television graduate programs have cropped up at universities across the country.

The thing is, my generation is different from Hollywood's previous generation, led by the likes of Barbra Streisand's hairdresser. We are the country's best and brightest. We come to the business from the top private colleges and the Ivy League. We are bona fide type-A's. Well groomed. We could have done anything. We could have gone to law school or medical school. We could have gone to Wall Street.

But, you see, we were raised on *Sesame Street*. We count *Star Wars* and *E.T.* as formative childhood experiences. Unlike our parents' generation, we have no Vietnam, no cause to bind us together. Instead we are bound by pop culture, by the movies we have all seen, by the TV we have all watched. We are the kids of the eighties. You know, the ones who played Space Invaders, wanted our MTV, and invented the Kevin Bacon game.

And as kids of the Reagan era we believed the feel-good trailers. Life as a John Hughes movie. Molly Ringwald is from the wrong side of the tracks but still gets the guy and such a fab prom dress. Ferris slides back into bed *just* in time. Anything is possible.

Go figure. We turned out to be young adults with a postmodern point of view. Witnesses to *Wag the Dog* in the wake of Monica L., watchers of both *The Truman Show* and the O.J. show, heirs to the (so-called) *Real World*. Life imitates art? *Please,* that is so *old*.

All right, here's what you've been waiting for. My parting advice for you out there ready to take your first plunge into showbiz: Your life is cinema. Some days are sheer comedy, others drama. There is a romance here and there, an occasional NC-17 night, and lots of adventure. What is important to remember is that you are the star. It is your picture. Go for it. Plop yourself down in an aisle seat. Get some Milk Duds and a Diet Coke. You will be on the edge of your seat. There will be thrills and chills and maybe some tears spilled. But I guarantee that the plot will be engrossing and the box office will (eventually) be optimal. Good luck!

talking the talk
(a glossary)

The movie business has a vocabulary entirely its own. It is a language of innuendo, a language of double entendre.

The following are words and expressions you need to know and understand in order to talk the Tinseltown talk.

above the line A production term denoting charges for story rights, the screenwriter(s), director, producers, and actors and all costs associated with them (including stunts, rehearsals, travel, living expenses, even personal trainers).

Acquisitions The area of the film biz that acquires the rights to distribute a movie from the makers of the film. A distributor may acquire domestic or foreign rights (or both). Such acquisition deals are usually struck for finished films, but may also be made on films in production or preproduction or ready to go into production. Indie films need to be acquired in order to "get out there" into the marketplace for the general public to see and in order to recoup their investors' funds. Acquisitions execs travel to film festivals around the globe looking for films to buy. The top three most important film festivals are considered to be:

Sundance—Park City, Utah, January

Indie-madhouse showcase, increasingly commercial, buzz here can make or break a film's chances for distribution. Perk: Ski between screenings.

Cannes—Cannes, France, May

Glitzy, glam film market extraordinaire punctuated by stars galore, black-tie *chaque soir.* Perk: Party till dawn.

Toronto—Toronto, Canada, September

Not as sceney as the above two but still a major movie marketplace. Perk: Canada?

Other important festivals include: Telluride, Berlin, Venice, and Seattle.

against You'll hear that a script went for a "low six-figure offer against mid-six figures." This means that the screenplay's actual purchase price was a low six-figure offer (let's say $150,000), but the writer will receive additional funds (let's say another $400,000), bringing the total to $550,000 or mid-six figures if and only if the movie is produced.

agents, agencies Agencies and the agents they employ are the primary suppliers of talent and material to the entertainment business. Agents act as salespeople on behalf of clients—actors, writers, and directors. They package and broker and negotiate deals, take care of travel and trailers and delicate egos for a 10-percent cut of each job procured. For example, if CAA's (see under the C's) adorable agent Patrick Whitesell sells clients Matt Damon and Ben Affleck's latest script—we'll call it *Good Will Fishing*—for $800,000, CAA would make $80,000 off his boys. The business and dough Patrick brings in is then reflected in his company bonus. Agents are who they represent; they're as important and successful as their clients. And agents (stars in their own right) often have an alliterated or rhyming name, or at least a name with a ring, a zing like: Bob "Bookie" Bookman (CAA), Mavis Davis (CAA), Amanda "Binky" Urban (ICM), Biff Liff (William Morris), and Boaty Boatwright (ICM).

Alan Smithee Hollywood's version of John Doe. It is the name directors or screenwriters (or on rare occasions actors) will use if they don't want to be identified as having been associated with a motion picture. Such distancing occurs, of course, when the movie is beyond bad. While a fantastic film has many proud parents, a forgettable flop is often an orphan. Here's an example of an imaginary incognito credit sequence—it hypothetically reads: "Andrew McCarthy and Jonathan Silverman, in *Year at Bernie's, An Alan Smithee Film.*"

A-list Movie stars who can be relied on for their multiplex bankability. While there are both male and female celebs with box-office power, it is the boys who are perceived to be able to carry a picture. The A-list is a constantly morphing group (depending on whose film is hot and whose is not), which includes at present: Tom Cruise, Leonardo DiCaprio, Jim Carrey, Harrison Ford, Will Smith, Bruce Willis, Robin Williams, Mel Gibson, Wesley Snipes, Jackie Chan, Tom Hanks, Sly Stallone, Arnold Schwarzenegger, Eddie Murphy, and John Travolta. These guys have such clout that Fox's chairman Bill Mechanic once said, "If Tom Hanks wanted to do the phone book, we'd probably do the phone book." As a result, male A-list stars command crazy, inflated, ridiculous, many $ million salaries (capping out at $20 mil), such as Sly Stallone's 1995 $60 million three-picture deal with Universal.

The A-list gals are the proven lady Actresses (that's a capital A) such as Barbra Streisand, Michelle Pfeiffer, Susan Sarandon, Angela Bassett, Julia Roberts, Kim Basinger, Whoopi Goldberg, Meryl Streep, Nicole Kidman, Jodie Foster, and Meg Ryan. Or they're the next wave, the ones with the cool names—Minnie, Winona, Gywneth, Liv, Jada, Uma, Mira, Salma, Cameron, Halle. While their paychecks are hardly shabby (Julia R. is up to $17 mil, and Jodie has a $15-mil price tag), they don't make as much money as their leading men. Hey, who says they don't possess as magnetic a box-office *je ne sais quoi* as the guys?

ankle Tradespeak for resigning or leaving a job of one's own free will.

arc The journey and transformation of a script's character. Or the movement of a script from beginning to end.

associate producer Is not, as an old joke goes, the only one who will associate with the producer. The associate producer is actually the most junior person on a production team receiving screen producer credit.

attach, attached A way for a star, director, or writer to "reserve" a project by expressing verbal interest, without legal commitment and often without a formal meeting with producers. The attaching process also helps a producer to put a project together, because name talent can attract other desirable talent during the Development stage. Let's suppose a script has been percolating at Paramount. Gus Van Sant attaches himself, and suddenly Al Pacino signs on, because he was a fan of *Drugstore Cowboy* and has been yearning to work with Gus ever since. Then, what do you know, none other than Julia Roberts attaches herself, since she's been hoping for years to have the chance to act beside the likes of Pacino.

At the End of the Day A frequently used Hollywood expression meaning "when all is said and done." "At the end of the day, I'd rather see Ashley Judd in the role, but if we have to settle for Naomi, then we will."

audience When considering a film project, executives always ask, "Who is the audience?" What they are really trying to figure out is: "Who is going to buy a ticket to this film?" "Is it a demographic that frequents movies in droves?" The audience for certain types or genres of movies obviously varies. To generalize, there are dick flicks—blow-'em-up block-

busters—and chick flicks—romantic comedies and love stories. A crossover audience can be achieved by theme (the
sports thrust of the character-driven relationship drama *Jerry
Maguire* helped to attract a male audience) or through casting (put Brad Pitt in a gory serial-killer picture like *Seven* and
hey, you'll get me in the theater).

The latest (1997) stats from the Motion Picture Associa-
tion of America show that 68 percent of the moviegoing audience is under age forty (this group makes up just 50
percent of the U.S. population) and that the majority of the
audience, 49 percent, is between the ages of twelve and
twenty-nine (a group accounting for merely 31 percent of the
population). Boys ages twelve to twenty-two are estimated to
be about a third of the entire moviegoing public and therefore the most reliable moviegoers on the planet. So Hollywood obviously relies heavily on teen and twenty-something
revenue. This is good news for young D's: Who better to
know how to tap into the mind-set of the most viable audience than someone who comprises it?

available/availability When a D inquires if a certain writer,
actor, or director is "available," she is asking not if he is single
but rather if he is free to work—or if the artist is otherwise
engaged, writing or shooting another film. Chance touches
every movie (just as fate influences romance). Your intended
one may be dating another woman—and your number-one
pick for a starring role may be committed to another movie.
You'll have to have another love affair and a different movie
star.

back end Is not Will Smith's cute little backside. It is the pay-
ment Will procures post–picture release. The profit is from

overseas distribution sales, toys, games, TV spin-offs, etc. The back end is separate from any up-front, straightforward salary or fee for producing or directing or acting.

back story The imaginary prequel to a script. D's will often ask writers about a character's back story (Where is he from? Was he a geek as a teenager?) as a way of helping to flesh out that character and make him as real as possible.

beats The pivotal, active moments in a plot that comprise a script and move its story from beginning to end. Here are the story beats of the first three minutes of *Austin Powers:*

1. The year is 1967: A certain Dr. Evil declares his determination to eliminate Austin Powers, the only man in the world who can stop his master plan.

2. We meet the studly ladies' man Austin Powers, who (after a musical interlude) receives a call from British Intelligence warning him of Dr. Evil's imminent trap at the Electric Pussycat Swingers Club.

3. At the club: Austin kills one of Dr. Evil's henchmen.

4. Dr. Evil cyrogenically freezes himself, shooting into space with the warning that he'll see Mr. Powers in the future.

been seen, been around Like a serial-dater-guy or a girl who is a little too familiar in certain circles, no one in Hollywood is interested in a script with a past, one that has been seen or been around, one that that has been checked out at production companies and studios previously. Whether or not executives initially expressed interest is not the point. The point is that the project is old news, not a fresh face in town.

below the line The production costs that are not above the line, such as production staff, set construction, grip and set operations, wardrobe, makeup, props, transportation, location or stage or back-lot charges, anything technical like lighting or special effects, editing, sound, postproduction lab charges, insurance, as well as publicity and marketing.

bid, bidding An offer on a script or a book. If more than one company intends to make an offer, producers or executives place bids with an agent for its rights. Sometimes the auction is a formal one: The agent announces that bids will be accepted via fax before a closing hour on a given day. Other times bidding will just spontaneously start. The agent brokering the deal keeps going back to each company by phone, driving the price up and up, until the highest bidder is victorious. In 1997 Nick Hornby's book *About a Boy* went to New Line Cinema for $2.75 million after four hours, leaving Miramax and Paramount in the dust.

box office aka B.O. Revenue as reported by movie theaters across the country. Note: A movie that grosses $50 million at the box office over a weekend has not made $50 million in profit. The "negative cost" of the film, including marketing, must be accounted for.

brass (top brass) Tradespeak for studio executives.

broad comedies Think general yucks. Mass chuckles. Sweeping silliness. Think *Airplane, Dumb and Dumber, Wayne's World,* or anything starring Adam Sandler or David Spade or Mike Myers.

brought in, bring in A production company brings a project (script, treatment, article, book) in at a studio. Studio execs then decide whether the project in question is worth their buying for that production company to produce.

buckslip Notepaper, made of a heavy stock, about six inches long and two inches wide, with the company logo and the exec's name on the bottom. Getting your first personalized buckslip is a career milestone.

the business Is there any other?

Buzz Hollywood hype. It is the word on the street about a hot or not script, feature, student film, performance, undiscovered star—you name it. Buzz reigns. Buzz can make or break a spec. Buzz can create a frenzy over an unread novel by an unknown first-time writer. Buzz can turn Sunday's nobody from nowhere into Monday's flavor of the week. And you don't have to be a publicist to generate buzz. An assistant or Development exec or an agent can spread buzz by vaguely mentioning to a fellow insider that they "heard Sherri Cooper's short, *Juliet Finkelstein Does the Hamptons,* has a lot of heat." Such a comment touches off a game of "telephone"—by eve, Sherri's name has been heard as Terri and Finkelstein has been distorted to Finkelberg—but filmmaker and film have landed on "edgy up-and-coming directors to watch" lists around town.

CAA CAA, Creative Artists Agency, is a powerhouse talent agency. The huge Lichtenstein in the lobby of its chic I. M. Pei–designed Beverly Hills digs sets the hard-core signature tone for clients strolling through, such as: heavy-hitters Antonio Banderas, Warren Beatty, Nicolas Cage, Michael Douglas, Dustin Hoffman, Anthony Hopkins, writer/director Cameron Crowe *(Jerry Maguire)*, author Michael Crichton *(Jurassic Park)*, and heavy-hitter-esses Helen Hunt, Nicole Kidman, and Amy Heckerling (writer/director, *Clueless).*

chaos theory A science invented by physicists that tries to find a pattern in inexplicably random things like the spread of disease, the weather, or the stock market. This mathematical model has been applied to the chaos of the Hollywood box office by theorists Art De Vany and David Walls. The scientists base their Hollywood application of chaos theory on the accepted notion that "nobody knows anything"—i.e., the movie business is totally random, it is impossible to predict box-office success even with high-concept films featuring major movie stars—as evidenced by flops like Schwarzenegger's *The Last Action Hero* and Stallone's *Daylight.*

commercial What sells to moviegoing audiences. What is perceived as commercial in Hollywood is constantly in flux. *Home Alone* makes zillions, and movies starring children are in vogue. Then Macaulay gets zits, and a string of not-as-successful live-action children's movies like *Dennis the Menace* or *The Secret Garden* come along. As a result, live-action kids' movies temporarily disappear. Another example: *Scream* "rediscovers" the teen horror genre, and *Scream 2, I Know What You Did Last Summer, I Still Know What You Did Last Summer,* and *The Faculty* follow.

completion bond A bond issued by a bank or completion-bond company, which provides completion insurance for an independent film. If the feature runs out of money in the course of production, the bond will supply the film's finishing funds.

Studio movies do not require completion bonds, because a studio assumes the film's financial risk and simply digs further into its bank-financed pockets if a project runs over budget.

Conference To connect a call with more than one person on the line. Most phone systems are set up to conference no more than six parties. If more people are involved, call AT&T at 1-800-232-1234, and they'll take care of it for you!

courtesy read A script read as a favor to someone.

cover, coverage Coverage is the grown-up's book report on a script. Written by a reader, it is comprised of a one-sentence log line, a two- to four-page synopsis, a page of comments (consisting of the reader's opinion of the merits of the material), and a verdict for executives: "recommend" (you've got a huge hit on your hands), "consider" (some issues need to be addressed, but the material is strong enough for you to transform it into film), "maybe" (you should take a quick look at the script, but it's highly doubtful), or "pass" (I think this script totally sucks and so will you). Coverage exists so that executives don't have to actually read material themselves.

creative meeting A Development-department meeting occurring two to three times a week. The object of these meetings is to share information on the status of projects in Development, as well as on new material that D's and execs have read, are looking at, or are looking for.

cross between A way of describing a project by relating it to other films. For example, I once pitched a romantic comedy called *I Saw U* to my superiors. The idea was based on a column of the same name in *The Stranger,* a Seattle newspaper. Basically, if you see the grungy, pierced chick of your dreams at Starbucks (and don't have the balls to talk to her), you can place a free "I Saw U" ad. Romance ensues. I characterized the movie as a cross between *Sleepless in Seattle* and *Desperately Seeking Susan.*

dailies (aka rushes) The production term for that day's footage—just processed and rushed from the lab.

delivered Turned in. A writer delivers the manuscript of his book to publishers, or a screenwriter delivers a draft of her screenplay to an executive.

(on his/her/the) desk An agent's assistant works on that agent's desk. This is not a literal "on," as in "on top of," mind you, but an imprecise "on," which should really be replaced with "next to." Nevertheless, the goal of a mailroom trainee is to get on a desk, or to be assigned to a specific desk, which means assigned to (or hired by) an agent and sitting in a cubicle in near proximity to his office.

Development hell The all-too-common phenomenon of a never-ending state of Development. A project in Development hell is usually troubled in some way or another: Perhaps a starlet was attached and backed out, or the producer was ineffective. Most commonly, though, the Development process is perpetuated by constant screenplay/story adjustments, changes, rewrites, and new writers. A project can be in Development for ten years, during the course of which ten writers, each of whom writes ten drafts, are hired and fired.

dictated but not read A common capital-letter disclaimer on the bottom of a letter. The disclaimer most frequently appears on a script-submission letter from an agent. "Dictated but not read" is an expedient way of imparting this message: "I'm a very busy person, far too busy to proofread this letter, and if your name is spelled wrong or if there is for that matter anything grossly inaccurate or offensive herein, my assistant is solely to blame."

discretionary fund A lump sum that production companies can use at their own discretion to purchase material—without their sponsor-studio's permission. It's basically play money, set aside.

edge, edgy Cool, hip, funky, fresh, new, different, button-pushing and jaw-dropping. Edgy material explores new territory and redefines the line of decency or indecency with regard to violence or sex or language or shocking subject matter. Independent films are usually edgy, while studio movies may try to be edgy (executives frequently evoke the word in describing what they're looking for) but rarely succeed. *Trainspotting* was edgy. Quentin Tarantino used to be edgy. David Lynch remains edgy. Films that were edgy in their day stand the test of time—films like *Easy Rider* (1969), *Blue Velvet* (1986), *sex, lies, and videotape* (1989), *Heathers* (1989), and *The Crying Game* (1992).

Endeavor Agency A top "boutique" agency formed by renegade ICM agents in 1995. Endeavor's stable includes top talent like Wes Craven, Kevin Smith, Edward Norton, Adam Sandler, Lisa Kudrow, Bette Midler, David Spade, and Parker Posey.

event movie More than a movie: an event, a cultural phenomenon. Larry K. And Dan R. And the *New York Times* Op-Ed page and your grandmother all have something to say about it. And if you haven't seen it . . . well, something is wrong with you. Think *Jaws* and *Star Wars* and *E.T.*, or *Jurassic Park* and *Independence Day* and *Titanic*. Event movies are usually huge-budget extravaganzas. But a movie can be an event because of exceptional critical revues or a cherished director (take *Saving Private Ryan)* or a political statement *(JFK)*. Sometimes a film is merely marketed as an event movie (complete with a premiere at Cape Canaveral and a number-one tune by Aerosmith) but never achieves true event status in society.

favor The planting of favors and repaying of favors is an essential part of doing business in *the* business. The most successful people in the entertainment business place favors purposefully and perfect the collecting of these favors to a high art: When information is shared on the down low, or a project is passed along, or an introduction made, the deed is prefaced by "I am doing you a favor"—a reminder that a day will come when reimbursement will be required.

first act, second act, third act The basic dramatic structure—beginning, middle, and end. As applied to a screenplay, the first act (roughly thirty pages) establishes the setup, the second act (about sixty pages) hashes out the conflict, and the third act (around thirty pages) finds a solution. It is helpful to think of the acts as: number one—*who* (is it about?); number two—*what* (happens?); and number three—*how* (is it resolved?).

(get) fucked Hundreds of execs get fucked multiple times a day in Hollywood. They get screwed by agents and producers and managers and other execs—by anyone and everyone. No, not literally! They get screwed in the *business* sense— screwed out of a script, a deal, a purchase price, a green light, etc.

galley A preliminary, bound version of a yet-to-be-published book—the phase between a loose manuscript and what you see on the bookstore shelf.

get into bed with Get into business with or make a deal with.

going out with (a script) Although it might seem as if D's date scripts, since they tend to spend so much time in sack with them, going out with a script is actually an agent's gig. When an agent sends a spec screenplay or a manuscript out to studios and production companies, she or he has gone out with that script. This submission may be prefaced by a phone call from the agent "I'm going out with . . . are you interested?" Or the D may call to request the script. The script might go to only one company for a first look, or it might be sent out wide to the whole town.

green light A green light is the signal of the end of Development and the beginning of production. It means the studio has agreed to, committed to, and given the go-ahead to make the movie. The authority to green-light a film equals real power in Hollywood. While many execs can say yes to buying a pitch or script, a mere handful at the top can say yes to endorsing the checks that set the production wheels in motion.

gross The studio's revenue stream for a movie, *before* distribution, expenses, interest, or negative costs are deducted. Specifically, gross is worldwide theatrical box office (minus exhibitor share), plus video sale and TV sale. Here's what a gross might look like: To make it neat, say a movie does $100 million at the box office. A studio sees roughly 42 percent, or $42 million (the rest goes to exhibitors), of that cash. It ships a hundred thousand video units at $30 a pop and makes a cool $3 mil. Then it sells free TV rights to a network for $12.5 million and pay-TV rights to cable for $3.5 million. Total gross: $61 million.

Adjusted gross is the gross, minus various points as negotiated. Generally adjusted gross is all or a percentage of negative costs (what it cost to make the film) and marketing and distribution costs. The lucky few who have the leverage to earn "gross-profit participation" (stars like Tom Hanks and Arnie S. And Sly) are actually receiving a percentage of the adjusted gross, not actual gross.

heat With enough buzz, a script, writer, director, actor, actress, or flick can be described as having heat, as in "she's got heat," "he's got heat," "they've got heat." D's are both heat-seekers and heat-generators.

helm, helmer Trade talk for to direct or a director.

high-concept An idea for a film that can be pitched in thirty seconds and described in less than a sentence. The most commonly referenced high-concept film is *Die Hard,* which spawned *Die Hard* in a Tunnel *(Daylight), Die Hard* on a bus *(Speed), Die Hard* on a boat *(Speed 2), Die Hard* on an asteroid *(Armageddon).*

High-concept action flicks are formulaic in structure. Here's a breakdown using *Con Air* as an example: The first act has some major crisis (a plane is hijacked by prisoners), the second act is a bleak one in which the hero is tested (Nicolas Cage can escape to his wife and child or stay on the plane, risking his life but fulfilling his obligation to justice), the third act is all about redemption (bad guys get their due, and father, wife, and child are reunited at last—stuffed animal and all).

"Redemption" is often pointed to as the essence of a high-concept feel-good character arc, as Sly Stallone quips in Joe Eszterhas's *Burn Hollywood Burn, An Alan Smithee Film:* "I believed in redemption for John Rambo, for Rocky Balboa, of course. I think that redemption is a good for the soul, it's good for box office, it's good for the country. It's a cleansing thing. It's a definite."

High-concept movies are not all action films, however. There are high-concept comedies as well: A divorced father denied custody disguises himself as a nanny to spend time with his children, starring Robin Williams *(Mrs. Doubtfire).* A man discovers his entire life is a sham lived inside a television show, starring Jim Carrey *(The Truman Show).* A grown guy can't inherit his money until he successfully completes each grade he has flunked, beginning with kindergarten, starring Adam Sandler *(Billy Madison).*

(the) hook The box-office draw—whatever it is that sets a movie apart from the pack and reels in an audience. The hook might be a marketing angle: "Come see the most expensive film ever made." The hook might be the casting: "Come see some of the finest actors of our time. Robert Downey, Jr., John Malkovich, Ralph Fiennes, and Harvey Keitel in . . ." The hook could be a director: "Come see Oliver Stone's latest and most controversial film yet." The hook could be a hit TV-show predecessor: "You love *The X-Files,* come see Mulder and Scully on the big screen." The hook can also be a genre, a sequel, or a prequel. And on rare occasions it's even just a really good, really original idea.

hot A script with buzz. An actor who's cute and sexy. An actress who's "in" thanks to a half-nude *Vanity Fair* cover and the right co-star. A director who's sought-after. Warning: The one who is hot today may be a proverbial flash in the pan, sure to be ice-cold tomorrow.

housekeeping deal A bare-bones deal wherein a studio or production company offers a producer the opportunity to "keep house" in their house. The boarder (who pays no room and board) develops projects with that roof-lending company's involvement in mind, and gets an office complete with phones, fax, and all that stuff.

ICM International Creative Management, a big name for a big agency that represents big talent on both coasts. ICM clients include the likes of actors Steve Martin, Julia Roberts, Sigourney Weaver, Courtney Love, Winona Ryder, Billy Zane, Richard Gere, Angela Bassett, Dennis Quaid, Geena Davis, Susan Sarandon, and Tim Robbins and directors

Spike Lee, Danny Boyle *(Trainspotting),* Mike Figgis *(Leaving Las Vegas),* Baz Lurhrmann *(Romeo and Juliet)* and screenwriters Joan Didion and John Gregory Dunne *(Up Close and Personal),* and Callie Khouri *(Thelma & Louise),* as well as authors Toni Morrison *(Paradise)* and Caleb Carr *(The Alienist).*

independent film/indie A movie made with independent (private investors') funds, rather than studio financing. Independent pictures are therefore movies that answer to nobody. They are films made by a filmmaker with a singular vision, rather than by a committee of executives.

Indie budgets are often closer to $1 million than their $100-million studio-rich relatives. But indie films are rich in spirit and in the ability to take more risks. The definition of independent film has become murky in recent years because Hollywood studios have bought or acquired independent companies like New Line (Time Warner), Fox Searchlight (Fox), Sony Pictures Classics (Sony), October (Universal), and Miramax (Disney), creating indie-studio hybrids that fall into neither category.

the industry Just as New Yorkers refer to Manhattan as "the city" (as though there were only one city in this vast nation), showbizzers refer to the entertainment industry as "the industry"—the only business that matters (at least to them).

ink(ed) To sign a deal.

internal (story) A story that takes place largely inside a character's head. Internal books are often about an emotional

journey—the sort that works well in a novel but is very difficult to translate visually to the screen.

leave word, left word The busy assistant's terse, succinct
phone code. Implicit in the phrase "so and so left word" is
"my boss would like to leave a message for your boss, and
could you please have your boss return the call?" On a
phone sheet the recording of such a left word is further con-
densed to "LW."

    The rules of Hollywood etiquette are that when one party
leaves word, the other should return the call. However, there
are no rules about returning and avoiding at the same time,
which is entirely possible between coasts. In fact, it is very
easy to *keep* leaving word, thus maintaining a friendly but pur-
poseful game of phone tag for weeks on end. The East Coast
simply leaves word for the West Coast before noon (which is
before 9 A.M. California time), or at 4 P.M. (lunchtime in L.A.).
The West Coast leaves word for the East Coast before leaving the office, around 6 P.M. (which is, of course, 9 P.M. in New
York City).

logline The one-sentence statement of the premise of a
script. The logline is part of a reader's coverage.

lot (studio lot) A studio's home—sort of like a big parking
lot for cars and sound stages and sets and offices and trailers. Lots are vast, with streets and alleys and many opportunities to become very lost. A map is helpful. When there's no
map to be found, however, there are always landmarks: "Just
turn left at the Yoda statue, then take a right after Homer
Simpson."

the majors The eight major studios: Columbia, Paramount, MGM/UA, Fox, Universal, Warner Brothers, Disney, and DreamWorks SKG.

manager If an artist is a corporation, then the manager is the CEO, overseeing and working with the whole team—from the artist's agent to lawyer, business manager to production company, publicist to stylist.

While there is overlap in what managers and agents do, there are fundamental differences: A manager usually takes a 15-percent cut of an artist's paycheck, while an agent gets 10-percent of a job procured. Managers have fewer clients, in theory giving each greater focus than an agent. Managers can produce movies and TV shows and can develop projects for clients—agents by law cannot produce. A manager's role is to be a career strategist and adviser, a long-term planner. Actors often hire managers to get them to a new place; to make a transition from music to film, from TV to film, from supporting roles to starring roles; to jump-start a stale career; or to keep them coasting on top.

manuscript The typed pages of an unpublished book. A manuscript might be a novel or a nonfiction work; it might be a partial (incomplete) or a draft or the final version. Manuscripts may or may not have publishers and/or publication dates.

meet-and-greet A type of meeting with no agenda other than to get acquainted and hear about one another's projects.

meeting (to take a) At a Hollywood party in Woody Allen's *Annie Hall,* there's a snippet of overheard cocktail chatter:

"Well, will you take a meeting with him?"

"I'll take a meeting with you, if you'll take a meeting with Freddy."

"I took a meeting with Freddy."

"Freddy took a meeting with Charlie. You take a meeting with him."

"All the good meetings are taken."

The absurd conversation comments on the politics of taking a meeting. Your place in the motion-picture-business pecking order is relative to whom you can and do and will take a meeting with (and who will take a meeting with you). In the Hollywood office, a D-Girl or Guy may take a meeting with the town's latest directorial find or young star, but rest assured that when Ron Howard or Sandra Bullock comes in for a chat, it will be with senior execs alone.

meets A way of describing a project, capturing its tone and sensibility by comparing it to movies past. I'll use the real example of a project that I helped to set up at MTV Films. Based on a book called *Getting into Yale: How One Student Wrote This Book (To Get into the School of His Dreams),* the movie idea is a high-school mockumentary, a send up of the whole getting-into-college thing—and I described it as *Waiting for Guffman* (the mockumentary part) meets *Welcome to the Dollhouse* (the quirky, offbeat, high-school part).

net (net profit) Producers must leap without a net. Net profits rarely materialize—even for films that gross hundreds of millions of dollars. After studio overhead is deducted (anything and everything under the sun from rent to salaries), studio accountants somehow find a way to make surplus profit vanish.

no talk no trade A request (often abbreviated to NTNT) registered in regard to a script snuck by an editor, slipped by a fellow exec, or lent by an agent that the surreptitious sharer wishes shared with no one else.

official An official submission is a submission from the agent who represents the work (rather than a copy of a copy borrowed from another production company, who borrowed it from a studio, who borrowed it from a producer, who got it officially).

one sheet A movie poster/advertisement (or a single-page statement of a movie concept—somewhere between a pitch and a treatment).

open To open is to open *big* at the box office. A big opening weekend translates into staying power—the key to profitability. If a movie does not open big, chances are that half its business will drop off by the next weekend and then it will get replaced in theaters the following weekend. Producer Robert Evans has famously equated the import of a film's opening to parachuting out of a plane: "If it doesn't open, you're dead."

A movie's soundtrack has become a major component of the blockbuster formula. A hit song and video on an endless MTV loop for the film's target audience is *free* advance press, advertising, marketing, and hype for a film. The ultimate example is the song "Men in Black" from the movie *Men in Black,* sung by the flick's star, Will Smith. The song, released a perfectly planned six weeks before the feature's all-important opening weekend, helped to drive ticket sales through the $51-million mark, the third-biggest opening of all time.

opened up When a story is too small for the big screen, there is still cinematic hope if it can be opened up—broadened to accommodate more characters, more locales, more universal themes, etc.

option, falling out of option Instead of buying rights to material outright, an option is paid on a project. An option is about 10 percent of the whole purchase price and lasts anywhere from six months to two years. An option gives a producer time to put a project together, reducing financial risk. When an option runs out, the optioner has the chance to renew for an additional sum; if a choice is made not to renew, the script has fallen out of option, meaning the rights are returned to the owner (who can option the project to someone else). However, if and when a project under option goes into production, a full purchase price is paid.

out on submission Describes a script that has been sent out by an agent and is in the process of being looked at by buyers.

package, packaging The writer + director + star(s). When a package is assembled by a producer or agent, the film has a stronger chance of finding studio backing and landing on the Development fast track.

partial Part of an unfinished book manuscript.

pass, a pass, to pass No, not making a pass *at* an agent! Passing *to* an agent—we're talking rejection of a submission. Passing well and politely is key, because you want the agent to keep feeding you scripts in the future. When you pass, try to think of something positive to say about the material, the writing, or a character and have an intelligent, thoughtful criticism as well as a concrete reason that the project isn't right for your company.

patch To connect an incoming call with a third party outside the office.

pay-and-play deal This guarantees a director, actor, or writer a chance to "play," a shot to practice their craft and prove themselves. According to such a deal, an artist who is at any point removed from the project is still to be paid in full.

pay-or-play deal This offers a set sum to be dispensed to a director, actor, or writer (who has made a pay-or-play deal), *whether or not* the film goes into production. While such a deal guarantees that the talent will get paid, it does not guarantee that they will have the chance to "play" on the film set. In other words, they may receive pay for no work!

phone sheet/phone log A phone sheet is the list of calls that need to be returned and placed. When stored in a notebook or on the computer, the collective record of these calls become a phone log. Phone-sheet calls are often color-coded with a highlighter. Here's the standard: Yellow = Left Word. Blue = Connected. Pink = Pending.

pick up/picked up (by a distributor) Being picked up by a distributor doesn't mean that Harvey Weinstein approaches you in a bar. What it does mean is that a company purchases the rights to distribute an independent film nationally and/or internationally.

pipeline All of a production company's or studio's projects in any stage (from those just optioned to those in Development hell to those green-lit) comprise the pipeline. Making movies is a crapshoot. Since it is so difficult to get films made and so difficult to predict which films will be box-office successes, the "throw enough shit on the wall and something's gotta stick" theory prevails. The idea is to fill up that pipeline with many more projects than will ever get made—and something is bound to come out the other end.

pitch A movie idea distilled into a brief sales speech. Legend has it that pitches should be twenty-five words or less, ideal for those notoriously short Hollywood attention spans. In Robert Altman's film *The Player,* the unwritten rule is used precisely by a tenacious screenwriting duo: "Bruce Willis sends Julia Roberts to the gas chamber. When he finds out she's innocent, he has to break into prison to save her life." (Go ahead, count those words.) Pitches are usually not quite so terse, however, often running ten to thirty minutes.

player A producer or an agent or an executive on the inside of Hollywood's power game. A dealmaker, an influence wielder, and a celeb in his or her own right.

polish Final, minor, superficial changes made to a good-to-go script.

preem The trades' word for a movie premiere.

preempt, preemptive bid A buyer's offer to purchase a project before other bids are entertained. Since it's an attempt to take the material off the market, a preemptive offer is usually fairly high. The catch is that the proposition is a strict, blind "take it or leave it." The agent cannot share the figure with competition to escalate the price.

prexy The trades' word for president.

producer(s) Businesspeople, dealmakers, financiers, creatives, organizers, and packagers—all at the same time. A producer may be the one who finds and options the film's concept or the one who finds its financing or both. A producer also manages and facilitates the project and all of its elements from beginning to end: from getting a script (and getting that script into shape) to enlisting talent, controlling production, arranging distribution, overseeing marketing, and policing the release. A producer on a studio film usually receives a fee of $200,000 to $750,000. If very good, and very lucky, a producer *may* make a picture or two a year.

proposal A detailed outline of a yet-to-be-written book. Usually book proposals are longer than five pages but shorter than a hundred.

punch up (a script) Add jokes or witticisms or love scenes to render a script funnier or spicier or sexier.

put on (a project) To be an exec assigned to shepherd a project through Development terrain.

reader (aka story analyst) A freelancer who reads screenplays and manuscripts and writes coverage on them for a living. For some, reading scripts is a career, and for others it's
an interim job or a way of breaking into the business.

reading An out-loud, unstaged reading of a play or
screenplay by actors. The point of a reading is often
to attract the attention of Development execs. A star may
be enlisted to lend validity to and ignite interest in the
script. Readings of projects already in Development are
also common. These readings are put on for the benefit
of the writer and Development execs, who can get a
fresh sense of the script's strengths and weaknesses by
hearing dialogue and jokes and how an audience
responds.

rep/repped A star, writer, or director's rep is not his sleazy
reputation but rather his (perhaps equally sleazy) representation—as in his agent, manager, and lawyer.

returning, return(ed) Forever economical and efficient, Hollywood assistants do not speak in full sentences on the telephone. Rather, assistants communicate in shorthand:
"Returning?" (i.e., "Are you returning my boss's call?") or
"Can she return?" ("Can my boss call you back when she's
available?").

re-up(ped) To re-sign a contract or a deal that is up for
renewal.

rewrite A second or third or sixteenth draft. When a screenplay is turned in to the studio and production company, it is

reviewed by members of the Development staff, who write script notes. These notes are compiled and given to the writer to do a rewrite. Typically scripts go through several drafts (although double-digit drafts are not uncommon). Depending on the writer's contractual arrangement and on the executive's satisfaction with that writer, the current scribe may take another crack at the script, or a new writer may be brought in to make these revisions. As a rule, screenwriters hate to rewrite, and Development execs are notorious for wanting to put their own stamp on a script by changing *anything,* from characters to plot to pure minutiae, thus the joke:

How many Development execs does it take to screw in a lightbulb?

Development-exec response: Well, does it really *have* to be a lightbulb?

Versus:

How many screenwriters does it take to screw in a lightbulb?

Screenwriter response: (with horror) Oh, no! You want to change the *light*bulb!!!!

rights A story belongs to someone: the person who wrote it or lived it. So whatever form it's in—whether it's a book, a play, a screenplay, an article, or a life story—you need legal permission, or the rights, to turn it into a movie. Purchasing or optioning rights can cost anywhere from one dollar to millions.

rolling calls Describes an executive zipping through calls (returning and placing) with an assistant, from the office, from the car, from the plane, from the manicurist, from virtually anywhere.

rough cut The rough draft of a film. The very, very first version, which is comprised of shots edited together in a linear fashion.

samples Screenplay-writing samples. These scripts might be previously produced, currently in Development, or never sold. Regardless, samples are intended to be read only as specimens of the screenwriter's skill, style, and voice. D's must constantly look at samples in order to expand their crucial mental reserve of new writers for projects.

schmooze(d) Noun and verb. Feel-good cocktail chatter, small talk, social talk, and business talk in one. In part schmoozing is about giving props, kissing ass, flirting, flattering. But the thing is, it's not about *them,* it's all about *you.* It's about getting what you want, getting what you need— whether that's an introduction or some information, whether it's building a new relationship or reinforcing an old one. If you wanna make it in the movie business, you need to be on the make. In an industry where important business can get done at 2 A.M. After too much champagne (and plenty else), you just cannot underestimate the power of the perfect schmooze.

script A general term for material—screenplay, manuscript, or play.

script doctor A pinch-hitter for a screenplay. Script doctors are hired close to production to punch up a script generally or to nail the opening, add jokes, revise structure, illuminate characters, enliven action, or stretch suspense specifically. Sometimes a number of script doctors will operate on a big-budget script. There are about forty top screenwriter MD's in Hollywood, who are paid up to *$200,000 a week* for their surgeries (which they perform anonymously, surgical masks intact).

script notes Detailed comments on a script in Development. Script notes are written by the project's studio and production-company execs (who compile one set of notes from the collective "we") and are given to the screenwriter for the next draft. There is no definitive format. Usually, though, script notes have a general overview paragraph on top in which D's say something positive ("We're off to a great start") and mention what the notes focus on ("We think some structural issues and character problems need to be addressed"). Next is a statement of broad-stroke areas to work on ("We want the tone to feel more clever, outrageous, and darkly sardonic"; "The protagonist should hit some deeper emotional notes throughout"; "The love story develops too slowly and isn't steamy enough"; or "The third act needs to have more suspense built in"). Last come the page notes, citing specifics. For example: "P. 64: Romeo's dialogue is too on the nose. Can't he seduce Juliet more subtly?"

Script notes are the English major's dream task. Well-written notes are a great way for a D to get herself noticed.

sellers Agents or writers with projects and talent to sell. *Buyers* are producers and studios who can shell out the cash to buy movie material.

set up (a project) Although not quite a date, we *are* talking about a match made with a sugar daddy. Producers are forever pimping for their films, hustling to fix them up with Mr. Cash—who is usually a studio. When you hear a production company's D say, "We have a movie set up at Universal, a couple at Miramax, and a few over at Warner Brothers," the reference is to these financial hookups.

SFX Scriptspeak for sound effects.

shelf, shelved A project at a dead end. Development (and Development hell) has ceased. The flicker of hope for such a dormant script lies in the chance that at some point, weeks, months, or years after it is shelved, it might be dusted off and put into turnaround.

shop, shopping (around) When an agent shops a script around, he's submitting it to various companies, letting D's browse and decide if they want to buy. When a production company shops a script around, they're submitting it to various studios to see if any are interested in purchasing it for that producer.

sign, sign with When talent makes a commitment to representation, they sign with a particular agent and agency.

slate The lineup of projects for production or release.

slip, slipped, got it on a slip Did an editor, producer, D, or screenwriter slip you tongue or just some paper? A slip is anything received on the sly, rather than submitted officially by an agent.

small Describes a story with a scope and scale that is too narrow to be considered cinematic. Plays, since they usually have limited locations and few characters, are often dismissed as "too small for the big screen." Every so often, however, a small gem makes it to theaters, like the love story *The Bridges of Madison County*.

soft The opposite of edgy. A script described as soft could be ordinary or bland or cheesy or dull or sappy.

space fone A super-sound-sensitive speaker phone used for conference calls. The space fone hears all—so don't whisper about that schmuck on the opposite coast on the other end of the line.

spec, a spec, on spec A completed screenplay that a screenwriter scribed on her or his own without a commitment from a buyer. Writing a hot, high-concept, original spec screenplay is a way for a young, unknown writer to break into the business. It is also a way to make a mint overnight. When specs ignite a bidding war, prices soar. Shane Black made a cool $4 mil for *The Long Kiss Goodnight*. Ron Bass (*Rain Man*) can get $1 or $2 mil. On average, however, specs sell in the $200,000–300,000 range.

story department Another name for a Development office.

studio Studios are the money, marketing, and management machines that get commercial pictures made. They are: Columbia Pictures, DreamWorks SKG, Walt Disney Pictures, 20th Century–Fox, Universal Pictures, Polygram Filmed Entertainment, MGM/United Artists, New Line Cinema, Paramount Pictures, and Warner Brothers. The studios are owned by humungo conglomerates, parent companies you've heard of, like Sony, Viacom, Seagrams, News Corp., and Time Warner, and they operate in large part through bank financing (Fox, for example, has a billion-dollar Citibank loan). A quintessential studio picture today conjures megabudgets, megagrosses, megasequels, and their accompanying theme-park attractions, toys, Happy Meals, and megahype.

submission This is when you let an agent tie you up—with a script, that is. An agent sends, or submits, a script to a D to read with a letter articulating whether it is a sample, a spec, a galley, etc.

table reading An unstaged reading of a script by actors literally sitting around a conference table.

take A point of view, a spin, a twist, an angle, an original way of looking at an idea and turning it into an idea for a movie. The ideas requiring a take are the ones that are not obvious movies—like an article with a germ of an idea, but no story, or a beautifully written but small book. Find a way to give that article a beginning, middle, and end or a way to open up that book, and you've got a take.

talent Actors, writers, or directors.

territory A studio or division within a studio. A territory is assigned by an agent to a production company for a submitted script. Let's say a production company is interested in optioning a script for which the agent has assigned Disney's Touchstone as the territory. The production company can bring that script in only at Touchstone—nowhere else. Other production companies will have been assigned *other* territories.

theatrical A picture's release in movie theaters constitutes its theatrical run and revenue. What a movie grosses theatrically excludes revenues from video stores, cable, and free-TV sales.

thesps The trades' word for actors.

thin Describes a script that is slight on story and/or substance.

top sheet A basic cost breakdown of the film, the top sheet is devised by the production staff after a script is completed.

tracking, to track Trading information on up-and-coming, hot—and not—books, scripts, and projects. D's track with fellow D contacts at other companies over the phone, on the Internet, or at monthly meetings. Tracking tips are jotted down in notebooks, input into computer systems, and output on lists and flowcharts. Tracking is serious business.

trade A script procured on the sly from another Development person at another company—in exchange for a similar slip. Trading book manuscripts is commonplace in NYC.

(the) trades The showbiz trade publications: *Daily Variety, Daily Variety Gotham, Weekly Variety,* and *The Hollywood Reporter.*

treatment An outline-pitch hybrid in narrative form. Treatments can be from about three to ten pages in length.

turnaround This is when a studio releases a script that is in Development hell or one that is going nowhere or one that is about to be shelved or one that is already on the shelf (or any combination therein) to its producer. Then the producers have a certain amount of time (usually a little over a month) to set up the script at another studio—and to return at least some of the money the studio spent on purchasing the script and during the Development process itself. An example of a turnaround success story was *The English Patient,* which was released into turnaround by Fox after casting disputes. The producers then walked over to Miramax and walked away with nine Oscars.

UTA United Talent Agency. Although smaller than the big-three agencies (William Morris, CAA, and ICM), UTA is home to plenty of stars, among them Jason Patric, Martin Lawrence, Lukas Haas, Ben Stiller, Jean-Claude Van Damme, Vince Vaughn, the Wayans brothers, Jennifer Lopez, Janeane Garofalo, Sandra Bullock, and directors Paul Thomas Anderson *(Boogie Nights)* and Joel and Ethan Coen of *Fargo* fame.

vanity deal A star's production deal with a studio. Production companies are set up for celebs to keep them happy and keep them in business with that parent studio. This is not to say that the actors concerned don't take their studio deals very seriously. For stars, having a production company is a way to assert more control—over their careers, over the selection and Development of projects, and over the actors and directors with whom they work. Many stars have turned what began as vanity deals into thriving and respected companies (Danny De Vito's Jersey Films, Jodie Foster's Egg Pictures, and Robert De Niro's Tribeca Productions among them).

vehicle A movie driven by a celebrity. A vehicle is designed to promote a star (and to provide that star with ample opportunity to shine and show off). Metaphorically think Vince Vaughn at the wheel of a custom Lamborghini (could you die?).

weekend read Weekend homework for the exec set—a Development ritual. At a Friday weekend read meeting, D's discuss the scripts they read during the week and what they'd like colleagues or superiors to look at for a consensus-building second opinion. The weekend is also a time to play catch-up, read samples, and peruse the big books or screenplays that agents slyly submit Friday at 6 P.M.—just to ensure that there will be no idle vegging Sunday afternoon.

William Morris Agency Founded back in 1898, William Morris is the original agency. A century or so later the agency boasts clients like Woody Allen, Alec Baldwin, Billy Bob Thorton, Minnie Driver, Emma Thompson, Mira Sorvino, George Clooney, Kate Winslet, Richard Dreyfuss, Sean Penn, John Travolta, Kevin Spacey, Christopher Walken, Jennifer Love Hewitt, Diane Keaton, and Salma Hayek. Need I say more?

the world The place where a film (or script) transports the audience. A film might take you to the world of the Dalai Lama or the world of the porn industry or the world of a Southern Baptist preacher or the world of Wall Street traders or the world of the mob. The world is the color and flavor and magic of the movies.